Africa's Indispensable Role

by

R.L. Worthy

KornerStone Books
6947 Coal Creek Pkwy
Suite 206
Newcastle, WA 98059
Ksbooks@execs.com

Published by

KornerStone Books
6947 Coal Creek Pkwy
Suite 206
Newcastle, WA 98059
Ksbooks@execs.com

Copyright ©2012 R. L. Worthy

All Rights Reserved. No part of this publication may be reproduced, stored in a retrieval system or transmitted in any form or by any means electronic, mechanical, photocopying, recording or otherwise, without the prior written permission of the publisher.

Design and Layout: KornerStone Books

Unless otherwise stated, all images courtesy of The Hall of Records - KornerStone Books ©

Printed in the United States of America

The First Edition

ISBN: 978-0-9727627-6-2

This is Dedicated to You

Preface:

During the 19th century, the accomplished British intellectual Sir Godfrey Higgins would remark: *"I think it right to make an observation upon an effect of prejudice, which has operated for the concealment of truth in modern times more than any other cause what-so-ever . . ."* As someone who has spent decades scrutinizing this allegation, not only was he right—the Christian Church of the West has been one of the offense's greatest culprits! Believe me, as a Follower of the Way, it brings me no joy to substantiate Higgins' accusation here. That notwithstanding, the 21st century, our ancestors, **_and the teachings of the Christ himself_**—demand we stop ignoring, **but address**, the elephant in the room: **Racism.**

Preface

Here is a rather common example of a racially erroneous Western biblical depiction. It is said to represent Moses pleading with the Hebrews in ancient Egypt. This particular illustration (*one of a countless number*) is over one hundred years old.

However, the glaring problem with this portrayal of Moses and the Hebrews in Egypt is that the ancient Egyptians were Black! Now if the ancient Egyptians

Africa's Indispensable Role

were Africans, *which they were*; and Moses was raised in pharaoh's palace <u>as royalty</u> for years unbeknownst to the king, or his priest—*it is rather obvious that <u>Moses could not have been Caucasian</u>*!

This photo is of a stone sculpture depicting a lovely noble Egyptian couple c.1200 BCE. As someone who has photographed Egyptian artifacts for decades, I can assure you that this rendering is racially and culturally accurate. The examination of genuine Egyptian artifacts, *from their naturally locking woolly hair to their actively-melanized skin*— eliminates all doubt about the racial identity of the ancient Egyptians: <u>Undeniably Black</u>!

Preface

Truth be told—the scriptures explain that Joseph, Moses, and the Apostle Paul were all, *by physical appearance*, mistaken for Egyptians; *<u>and, in the case of Joseph, this was by his own brethren</u>*—but I digress. Here is a stone bust of an ancient Carthaginian nobleman. There is no doubt that the Carthaginians were Black because they often celebrated their Hametic heritage! Although many works of art from the Old World have been intentionally damaged to becloud the racial identity of the person—this artifact has survived to reveal this nobleman's true physical character. This bust is on display in the Bardo Museum in Tunis.

Africa's Indispensable Role

Listen, we could go on forever looking at genuine historical artifacts that prove the ancient Egyptians, Phoenicians, and Carthaginians were Black (*I have personally witnessed and documented thousands*). Yet and still, the point that needs to be made here is that the habitations of the Hebrews, and earliest Christian hubs for that matter, were predominately inhabited by Blacks—*not Caucasians!* A point clearly understood, and expressed here, by the 11th century creator of the Menologion of Basil II.

This painting is of the heralded Saint Gregory Thaumaturgus ("the Wonderworker"). He was born in Anatolia (Asia Minor) in the 3rd century CE.

Preface

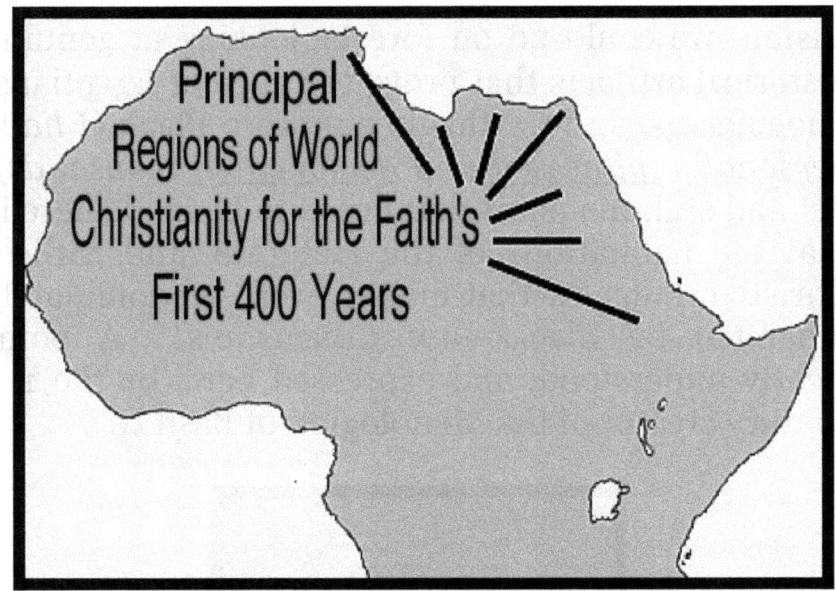

That all notwithstanding, here is a map of the major areas of Christian worship in Africa during the Faith's first 400 years. Africa was home to millions of Christians before the 5th century CE. Incidentally, the fact that the continents of Asia and Europe are not shown here is not an oversight, but a conscious decision. You see, **the tally of early Christians in Africa would easily dwarf the sum of the Christians of Asia and Europe put together**!

The historical record is clear: during the initial centuries of Christianity—Africans did not merely embrace the new religion—they would suffer tremendously for it. What's more, had it not been for the spiritual conviction of the people of the Nile Valley and Northern Africa—the very survival of the Faith must be called into question!

Africa's Indispensable Role

Conversely, the vicious malefactor of the Christian Religion during its embryonic stages on this planet, was none other than Europe's Roman Empire: **_actually murdering African Christians for hundreds of years_**. Fearful of people whose minds they could not control—Rome's emperors would carry out the most shameful campaign of savagery, _against the defenseless_, in human history!

Diocletian ruled Rome from c.284 – 305 CE. He would oversee the murder of hundreds of thousands of African Christians during his reign. This bust is kept in the Istanbul Archeological Museum.

Preface

For so much as I am not a racist, I have not merely written <u>Africa's Indispensable Role</u> for African Christians. It has been penned for Christians, and non-Christians, of all hues. Thus, if you are a person of sound character and intellect, it is my hope that this book will help to increase your understanding of the historic contribution made by Africans to the early Faith! In closing, the brilliant North African theologian Saint Augustine taught, *"all sin is a kind of lying."* If you agree, it only follows that Christians who acquiesce to liars are, *in a manner of speaking*, betraying the trust! Not only that—*in this instance they sully the memory of all those selfless African souls who gave their lives, so that they, and others, would achieve salvation . . .*

This is the ancient Egyptian Coptic Monastery of St. Simeon (near modern Aswan). It dates back to the epoch of the life of Saint Augustine.

CONTENTS

Dedication	v
Preface	vii
Table of Contents	xvii
In the Beginning	1
Saint Mark	6
The Early Proliferation of the Faith in Egypt	11
The 3rd Century Church in Africa	17
Africa & the Written Word	23
Pergamos	31
Christianity in Ethiopia	42
African Martyrs & Standard Bearers of the Early Faith	51

CONTENTS
{cont}

Constantine & Christianity in Europe	84
The Blossoming of Christianity in Ethiopia	103
Epilogue	118
Language Chart	122
Photo Credits	123
Bibliography	127
Index	139
Tribute	148
Notes	150
Saint George	152

In the Beginning

In the Beginning

While the surviving record of Christianity's early centuries is a bit fragmented—archeologists, historians, and biblical scholars all acknowledge the crucial role that the Africans of the Nile Valley played in the establishment of the new Faith! In brief, shortly after the Christ's crucifixion, the Apostles are reported as traveling to the far away Asian and European regions of Anatolia, Greece, and Italy; yet, their new Christian teachings were not well received by the peoples of those lands. As a matter of fact, the Apostles routinely faced open hostility.[1]

However, the nearness of the African Continent to Palestine, the large populations of Jews already living in the Nile Valley—and the African peoples' timeless affinity for true spiritual teaching and religious devotion, would all help to facilitate the early adoption of the Christian Religion in Africa![2]

---

[1] Cox, G., African Empires and Civilizations p. 99 & Burkill, T., The Evolution of Christian Thought p. 25
The term *Apostle* is derived from the Greek word Apostolos meaning, "To Send Forth."

[2] Rogers, J.A., Sex and Race Vol. I, p. 282 & Budge, E.A., Egypt pp. 146 - 147 & Burn, A., & Selincourt, A., Herodotus: The Histories p. 143 & I John 2: 7 - 11
The heralded Greek historian Herodotus considered the ancient Egyptians to be the most spiritual people on the earth. Furthermore, the concept of monotheism was not new to the spiritual hearts of the Africans of the Nile Valley. One clear illustration of this is Pharaoh Akhenaten's conversion of

Africa's Indispensable Role

This is a map of Egypt and Israel during the life of the Christ. As we all know, Israel's eastern and western borders have undergone many changes through the ages; yet, it is clear that Israel's southern border has always been adjoined with the African State of Egypt. Little wonder that the noted Roman historian, Gaius Cornelius Tacitus, should have no compunction about identifying the ancient Hebrews as, *"Ethiopians"* (Black people) in his celebrated 1st century chronicle, The Histories.

Egypt to monotheism during the 18th Dynasty: this was 14 centuries before the birth of Christ. In actual point of fact, the renowned Saint Augustine of Hippo would go so far as to explain: *"What is now called the Christian religion has existed among the ancients and was not absent from the beginning of the human race until Christ came in the flesh from which time the true religion which existed already began to be called Christian."* We even find the 2nd Chapter of I John stating: *"this is not a new commandment that I am writing to tell you, but an old commandment that you were given from the beginning . . ."*

In the Beginning

According to the Reverend Dr. Robert Taylor, <u>the first Christians were Hebrew Essenes who lived in Egypt</u>! Harnack supports Taylor's assessment when he explains that a greater number of Jews converted to Christianity in Egypt, than anywhere else during the religion's early years. These observations notwithstanding, the number of native Egyptians who embraced the Faith in the generations after the crucifixion grew to such an extent that they would soon establish their own Christian communities in the Nile Valley.[3]

Eventually coming to be known as the *Copts*, these devout Africans would undertake many treks to the holy lands in Israel. Indeed, once a year the Arch Bishop of the Copts of Dumyat undertook a great ceremonial pilgrimage from Egypt to Jerusalem. Moreover, many of these African Christians are

---

[3] Groves, C., <u>The Planting of Christianity in Africa</u> Vol. I, pp. 36 - 39 & Harnack, A., <u>The Mission and Expansion of Christianity in the first three centuries</u> Vol. II, pp. 91 - 92 & Higgins, G., <u>Anacalypsis</u> Vol. II, p. 43 & <u>The Coptic Encyclopedia</u> Vol. II, pp. 447 – 449, Vol. III, pp. 925 - 926 & Case, S., <u>Evolution of Early Christianity</u> p. 78 & Trigg, J., <u>Origen</u> p. 10 & Budge, E.A., <u>The Nile</u> p. 313 & Hall, M., <u>The Secret Teachings of All Ages</u> p. CLXXVIII

An aspect of the Essenic influence in Egypt is probably to be garnered from the finding that many of these early Christians prayed seven times daily: before sunrise; 9 am; 12 noon; 3 pm; 5 pm; 6 pm; and midnight. Later, Christians of 3rd century Alexandria would pray three times daily facing East with their arms outstretched (see page 5).

Africa's Indispensable Role

reported as taking up permanent residence in Israel.[4]

This is a stone relief of an ancient Egyptian Coptic woman with outstretched arms. Many African artifacts like this date back well before Rome's conversion to Christianity in the 4th century CE.

---

[4] Ibid.

Saint Mark

Africa's Indispensable Role

If the truth is to be told here, <u>the early Faith was not received anywhere in the Old World as well as it was amongst the Africans of the Nile Valley</u>! Ancient chroniclers tell us that Christianity began to take a firm hold in Egypt as early as the 1st century CE.! According to Church Fathers, the Apostle Mark founded the Church in Egypt c.61 CE. **NOW WHAT IS SO INCREDIBLE ABOUT THIS FINDING IS THAT THIS WAS OVER 250 YEARS BEFORE THE ACCEPTANCE OF CHRISTIANITY IN EUROPE BY THE ROMAN EMPEROR CONSTANTINE!**[1]

Allow me to share this rather extraordinary account of the events that led up to the Apostle Mark's establishment of the Christian Church in Egypt:

> *"Towards the evening, the strap of his sandal was torn, and he turned to the first cobbler's shop. As the cobbler was working, the awl pierced his hand, and he lifted it up, exclaiming: 'O One God!' Immediately the Apostle took some clay, spat on it and applied it to the wound, this healing it . . . taking his clue from the cobbler's exclamation, he started talking to him about God the Father and of His Son Jesus the Christ. The cobbler's heart was opened, and he took the Evangelist*

---

[1] Constantine, <u>Encyclopedia of Religion</u> Vol. IV, p. 70 Christianity was not considered to be a reputable religion by any of Rome's Emperors before the 4th century CE.

Saint Mark

to his home . . . That day, the seed of the good news was sown, and like unto the mustard's it grew in time into a mighty tree. Anianus, the cobbler, and all his household were baptized—becoming the first fruits of the Church founded by St. Mark . . . As the number of people joining the Faith continued to increase, the [Roman] authorities sought to lay hands on the Apostle. When the brethren heard of it, they pleaded with St. Mark to leave Egypt . . . Thereupon, he gathered the believers together, and ordained Anianus Bishop for them, and ordained with him, twelve priests and seven deacons. To these, he entrusted the direction of the church . . . During the Apostle's absence, Anianus and his helpers continued his work . . . The whole Christian community, at an early age, lived more or less a communal life, sharing everything together: praying, fasting, and preaching the word. The number of Faithful kept growing . . . As soon as St. Mark returned, they sought him, and eagerly asked him to write down for them the teachings of the New Way. Thus, in answer to their quest, and by the inspiration of the Holy Spirit, the Gospel according to St. Mark was written."[2]

---

[2] Metzger, B., The Early Version of the New Testament pp. 99 - 100 & Parrinder, G., Religion in Africa p. 101 & Griggs, C., Early Egyptian Christianity: From its Origins to 451 C.E. pp. 17 - 20 & De Graft-Johnson, J., African Glory

Africa's Indispensable Role

This is the ancient Coptic Cross of Egyptian Christianity. It is the universal symbol of the world's oldest Church that was founded in Africa by the Apostle Mark.

p. 39 & De Ferrari, J., The Fathers of the Church: Eusebius Pamphili-Ecclesiastical History Bks. I - V pp. 110 - 111 & The Coptic Encyclopedia Vol. I, p. 245, Vol. V, pp. 1529 - 1531 & Harnack, A., The Mission and Expansion of Christianity in the first three centuries Vol. II, p. 162 & Coptic Church, Encyclopedia of Religion Vol. IV, p. 82 & Misri, I., The Story of the Copts pp. 13 - 16, 23 & Cox, G., African Empires and Civilizations pp. 117 - 118, 120 & Philip, Illustrated Dictionary & Concordance of the Bible p. 785 & Hansberry, L., Pillars in Ethiopian History pp. 62 - 64 The Apostle Mark was the child of a well-to-do Hebrew family of Cyrenaica Africa. After becoming a Disciple in Israel, Mark returned to his native continent to preach Christianity to scores of receptive Africans in Cyrenaica and Alexandria as early as c.50 CE.—hence, his being accredited with establishing the first Church by Christian historians! Parenthetically, it should be noted here that Philip the Evangelist is heralded for converting and baptizing a Jewish Treasurer of the Queen of Ethiopia during the 1st century CE.

Saint Mark

In an effort to stop the expansion of Christianity in Egypt, a mob killed Saint Mark in Alexandria c.68 CE. A church known as *Bucalis* is purported to have been built on the very site in Alexandria where the Apostle was martyred. But Saint Mark's death did not serve his murderers well. In truth, his martyrdom would fuel the spread of his testimony about Christ and salvation! Shortly thereafter, it was determined that the Head of the Alexandrian Church should be the Patriarch (venerable Head) of all of Egypt's 1st century churches. Thus, the Apostle Mark is seen as the first in a long line of Nile Valley Church Patriarchs: <u>a tally that numbers in the hundreds and is celebrated to this day!</u>[1]

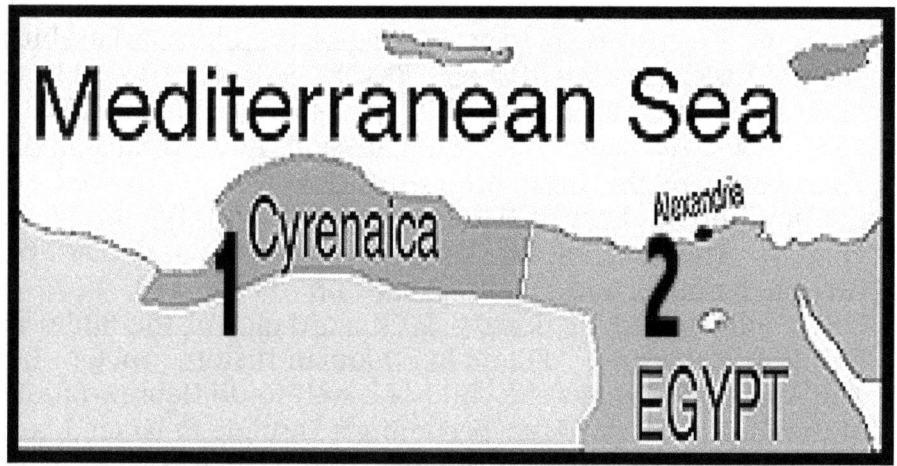

Map of the African regions of Saint Mark's birth (1) and his extraordinary 1st century ministry and martyrdom (2). One of the most celebrated portrayals of this Apostle can be seen on page 149.

---
[1] Misri, I., <u>The Story of the Copts</u> pp. 13 – 16, 23, 563 - 566

The Early Proliferation of the Faith in Egypt

Early Proliferation in Egypt

Researchers have not simply relied on historical accounts about the deeds of St. Mark to demonstrate the early gravity of Christianity in Egypt. They have also been able to corroborate the Faith's presence and growth through the unassailable record of Africa's Christian institutions, Christian literature, and the ancient archeological record! For example, the heralded Catechetical Institute, <u>considered to be the world's first great center of Christian scholarship</u>, was formed in Egypt during the 1st century CE. Founded c.60 CE. by Saint Mark, the mission of this African university was to have its clergy instruct novices in the doctrine of Christianity. The institute's curriculum would include the following subjects: the Godhead; the virgin birth; the crucifixion and resurrection; the Holy Spirit; the Second Coming; and the human body and soul.

Before long, this African institute was considered to possess the world's finest Christian minds. Frankly, the university dean's list reads like a Who's Who of the early Christian World: the first dean of the Catechetical Institute was Athengoras (who was a teacher of both Pantaneus and Clement); the second dean of the institute was Justus; the third head of the university was Eumanius; with Marianus serving as its fourth. While many men of stellar character and intellect would lead, and attend, this unrivaled African institution—I want to stop here to

Africa's Indispensable Role

say a brief word about a contribution made by two of the institute's pupils, *and champions*, of the early Faith; namely, Pantaneus and Clement.

This is a chart of the ancient Coptic Alphabet.

It was Pantaneus and Clement who created Egypt's Coptic Script in the 2nd century CE. In actual point of fact, the importance of this achievement to early Christianity is inestimable since its creation made the scriptures more accessible to the average Egyptian. Fast forward to 10th century feudal

Early Proliferation in Egypt

England for example; this was a time and place where 99 percent of the people still could not read Christian scripture, *even **if** they received access to it*, because it was written in a foreign tongue. But unlike most of Europe for over a millennium, the common people of the Nile Valley were able to read the Word centuries earlier because of the keen inventiveness of Pantaneus and Clement! In the words of Iris Habib Misri:

> *"Meanwhile, the leaders of the Church felt the need of having the Gospel written in the native tongue of the land, but in a script that would be within the grasp of the common man . . . According to tradition, Pantaneus and Clement cooperated to produce this new and easy script . . . the fruit of their labour was the Coptic language: namely, the pharaonic speech written in the Greek alphabets with the addition of seven letters for sounds which did not exist in Greek, but existed in Egyptian . . . Having given the Egyptians this invaluable gift of a simplified method of reading and writing, Pantaneus and Clement crowned their works with yet one grand service: they translated the Bible, both Old and New Testaments into Coptic . . . [These Africans] were the first scholars to translate the Scriptures, in their entirety, into their own native tongue."*[1]

---

[1] Groves, C., The Planting of Christianity in Africa Vol. I, pp. 36 - 39, 49 & Misri, I., The Story of the Copts pp. 23 - 25 &

Africa's Indispensable Role

Truth be told, a countless number of historians have made the point that the early Christian World's first beacon of brilliance and stability, was Africa's Catechetical Institute! As one scholar would put it:

"They realised that if they were to convince and win men deeply learned in all that was highest and best, they had to be just as learned and more erudite. To help them attain this erudition, St. Mark had opened for them the Catechetical School . . . During the first two centuries, catechetical schools were opened throughout different countries . . . These schools, however, exercised a very limited influence; they offered only an elementary catechism to pagans and new converts alike. But, in Alexandria, the matter was altogether different. Its school soon

---

De Graft-Johnson, J., African Glory p. 39 & Harnack, A., The Mission and Expansion of Christianity in the first three centuries Vol. II, pp. 157 - 158, 163 & Catechetical School of Alexandria, The Coptic Encyclopedia Vol. II, pp. 469 - 471, Vol. III, p. 900 & Rogers, J.A., Sex and Race Vol. I, p. 95 & Jongeling, K., & Kerr, R., Late Punic Epigraphy p. 10 & Hamilton, E., Mythology pp. 254 - 256

Incidentally, it was actually the ancient Canaanite script that was the basis of the later Greek alphabet. However, Clement of Alexandria followed Pantaneus as head of the institute c. 190 - 204 CE. Carrying on robustly for several years without a formal leader, in 215 Demetrius appointed the brilliant Egyptian Origen to lead the Institute. The influence of the university would not wane until the 5th century CE. The Egyptian Didymus the Blind is generally seen as the last heralded Dean of the Institute (born c.313 – died c.398 CE.).

Early Proliferation in Egypt

became the center of an intense intellectual life. The teachers who taught there were well versed in Hellenistic Literature and philosophy as well as the holy books bequeathed to the Church by the Synagogue . . . Little wonder, then, that the School of Alexandria became the Lighthouse of Christianity, and throughout its life of five centuries, it maintained its reputation of erudition and scholarliness."[2]

Ancient Coptic Christian wood carving of Christ (center) flanked by two angels. This artifact is housed in the Egyptian Coptic Museum in Cairo Egypt.

---

[2] Misri, I., The Story of the Copts p. 23

The 3rd Century Church in Africa

The 3ʳᵈ Century Church

Continuing on, religious scholars have also been able to make important historical determinations about the ebbs and flows of the early Faith from accounts of the lives of several of Africa's Church Fathers. For instance, the episcopate of Demetrius in Alexandria reveals that his tenure was a period of rapid expansion for Christianity in Egypt. Further, modern chroniclers have been able to verify that from his station he held sway over the policy of the Church in Alexandria! Additionally, we find that during this era the number of Christian bishops jumped from four to twenty-three, which clearly reveals the proliferation of churches in Northern Africa during the late second to early third centuries.[1]

Frankly, Africa is home to scores of the world's oldest and largest churches; a rather astonishing fact considering the ominous generational threat posed by the Romans. But the evolution of this phenomenon was probably something like this: the first places of worship were probably catacombs

---

[1] Livingstone, E., The Oxford Dictionary of the Christian Church p. 468 & Groves, C., The Planting of Christianity in Africa Vol. I, pp. 36 - 39, 49 & Misri, I., The Story of the Copts p. 23 & De Graft-Johnson, J., African Glory p. 39 & Harnack, A., The Mission and Expansion of Christianity in the first three centuries Vol. II, pp. 157 - 158, 163 & Catechetical School of Alexandria, The Coptic Encyclopedia Vol. II, pp. 469 - 471, Vol. II, p. 900 & Rogers, J.A., Sex and Race Vol. I, p. 95

Africa's Indispensable Role

and/or small private residences; next, as the number of Christians grew and the smaller homes could no longer accommodate the congregation, the conversion of the larger homes of some of the wealthier converts would have occurred; finally, outgrowing those dwellings—the Christian assembly would have built a church, or converted the site of an older religious temple to a house of worship.

Here is the entrance to an ancient catacomb. Located in Carthage, there is a very high probability that this catacomb would have served as a secretive site of assembly for many 2ⁿᵈ and 3ʳᵈ century Carthaginian Christians. *I hope you are beginning to understand that life for the first Christians wasn't about nice automobiles and/or playing bingo. We owe them a tremendous debt . . .*

The 3ʳᵈ Century Church

This is the exterior of an ancient Coptic church in Egypt. Note the Star of David (upper-center) between the two 12-pointed stars. The 12-pointed star could be used to symbolize either the 12 apostles or the 12 tribes of Israel.[2]

---

[2] Misri, I., The Story of the Copts & Alexandria, Historic Churches in, The Coptic Encyclopedia Vol. I, pp. 92 - 94 & Du Bourguet, P., Early Christian Painting pp. 7 - 9 & Du Bourguet, P., Early Christian Art p. 32, 40 & (Video), Behind the Veil: Nuns 1984 & Rogers, J.A., Sex and Race Vol. I, p. 281 & Clegg, R., Mackey's Revised History of

Africa's Indispensable Role

Early Notable African Churches

St. Mark's Church (known as Bucalis) was built on the Alexandrian seashore c.61 CE.

The Church of Our Lady was built c.264 CE.

The Church of the Virgin Mary was built c.282 CE.

The Church of Cosmas and Damian was built c.284 CE.

The Church of the Arch Angel Michael was built c.312 CE.

The Cathedral of the Jacobites was built c.318 CE.

Freemasonry & al-Makarim, A., Tarikh al-Kana'is wa-al-Adyirah

Demetrius lived from c.189 - 232 CE. A catacomb is an area of subterranean passages—which may, or may not, contain tombs. Also, it must be noted that unlike this age, during the early centuries of Coptic Christianity—the Hebraic and Christian religions had a great deal of respect for one another. In fact, it was not uncommon to find Coptic churches exhibiting Hebraic and Christian symbolism. For example, these Christians are known to have openly used the Star of David to express the divine and human natures of the Messiah. The obvious reason for this was because many of Africa's early Christians were Hebrew converts. Incidentally, the most famous Hebrew convert to trumpet the Messiah's coming was the prophet depicted on page 138 of this text.

The 3rd Century Church

These are ruins of the 3rd century CE. Basilica of Saint Cyprian in Carthage of North Africa. This is the location where the Saint was martyred. Modern day Carthage is located in the state of Tunisia.

Africa & the Written Word

Africa & the Written Word

It just so happens that another revelatory area of inquiry, *as to the religion's early development*, rests in the record of its spiritual documents. As for the significance of the historical study of Africa's ancient Christian literature—allow me to share this remark by Charles Groves:

> *"The use of Egyptian language by the Church is decisive evidence of its expansion among the original Egyptian population of the Nile Valley . . . when the Christian message reached . . . the original Egyptian inhabitants, some translation of the New Testament books was required. Of the native Egyptian dialects in use, three became the media of the new versions of the scriptures . . . of the native dialects in use . . . the Sahidic [tongue of the Upper Egyptian Kingdom] is the version regarded as the earliest . . ."*[1]

So as to avert any confusion, the Holy Books of the Christians of the 1st and 2nd centuries would have been the Hebrew <u>Pentateuch</u> (Torah) and later the <u>Septuagint</u> Bible. The Pentateuch was made up of

---

[1] Groves, C., <u>The Planting of Christianity in Africa</u> Vol. I, pp. 36 - 39 & Coptic Versions of the Bible, <u>Universal Standard Encyclopedia</u> Vol. VI, p. 2007 & Metzger, B., <u>The Early Version of the New Testament</u> pp. 103, 106 - 107

Bell echoes this sentiment when explaining: *"This evidence seems to justify the inference that even in the second century the number of Christians in Middle Egypt was by no means negligible and by the middle of the third was considerable."*

Africa's Indispensable Role

the first five books of the Bible: <u>Genesis</u>, <u>Exodus</u>, <u>Leviticus</u>, <u>Numbers</u>, and <u>Deuteronomy</u>. The <u>Septuagint</u> Bible was a compilation of Hebrew scripture that was translated into Greek, by Jewish rabbis in Africa, c.250 BCE.

These are a few fragments of the world's oldest <u>Septuagint</u> manuscript. Known as the Rylands Papyrus 458, these biblical passages are from the <u>Book of Deuteronomy</u>. The papyrus was discovered in Fayyum Egypt and dates back to the 2nd century BCE.

Africa & the Written Word

Modern day Christians have little trouble recognizing the Septuagint Bible as the Old Testament. The term *Septuagint* means, "Translation of the Seventy." According to Schwartz:

> *"The Septuagint is the Greek version of the Hebrew Old Testament; it was made in Egypt. The Pentateuch was probably translated in the 3rd century B.C., the other parts of the Old Testament in later times . . . The so-called Aristeas Letter describes how the Hebrew Old Testament, more exactly the Pentateuch, was translated into Greek [by 72 translators in 72 days] . . . at the time of [Egypt's] King Ptolemy II Philadelphus (285 – 246 B.C.)."*[2]

---

[2] Metzger, B., The Early Version of the New Testament p. 102 & The Septuagint Bible & Bible Translations, Ancient, Illustrated Dictionary & Concordance of the Bible pp. 181 - 184 & Schwartz, W., Principles and Problems of Biblical Translation pp. 17 - 19

The Ptolemies are purported to have been curious about the spirituality and culture of other peoples. The choice of making a Greek translation had little to do with the peoples of Greece: the Ptolemies, after all, were actually from Western Asia. Yet, after the spread of Hellenism during the life of Alexander the Great, we find that the Greek language began to be more widely used. It is further to be noted that after the elders of the Hebraic community examined the Septuagint text—they enthusiastically endorsed it and pronounced a curse upon anyone who altered the translation. Metzger explains that the Septuagint was utilized by African Christians as early as 90 CE.

Africa's Indispensable Role

However, as Christianity became a more established religion in North Africa, this Hebraic and Septuagint scripture (*commonly used by early Christians as a testament of the Messiah's coming*) began to give way to what must be deemed the world's first truly **Christian** record; namely, scriptures which addressed events in the life of the Messiah; the teachings of his Apostles; and revelations in the Faith! In actual point of fact, the first compilation of scripture that can be seen as the **New Testament** was not assembled until 185 CE. It is from this period forward that the Old and New Testaments were compiled and deemed to be the religion's canon scriptures.

I should further comment that the canon scriptures of these African Christians of the forefront were markedly different from the New Testament of today. In truth, the earliest generations of Christians used many scriptures that are not widely acknowledged in these times: e.g., I Infancy; The Book of Enoch; The Book of Jubilees; The Gospel of the Egyptians; The Gospel of Thomas; The Kerygma of Peter; The Synodicon; The Didascalia Apostolorum; The Gospel of Philip; The Testament of Our Lord; The Epistle of Barnabas; The Qalementos; The Shepherd of Hermas; and The Acts of John to cite a few.

Permit me to further explain that many of the accounts in these scriptures are fascinating. For instance, in <u>I Infancy</u> we are told of the Messiah's early life in Egypt: Mary and Joseph moving there to insure their child's safety. This book discusses Christ's life in Memphis and Thebes—and several of the miracles that he performed as a child. What's more, the Book of <u>Nicodemus</u> details the odd and frightening occurrences that took place immediately following the crucifixion. The text even explains that shortly afterwards, Pilate convened the heads of the Hebrew governing body in hopes of coming to terms with those events. Incredibly, these scriptures go on to say that after the Hebrew elders re-investigated the teachings of Michael in the first 70 books—and correlated that information with the dimensions of the Ark of the Covenant—the Hebrew elders would confess to Pilate that **the man they executed had indeed been their Messiah**![3]

---

[3] Ackroyd, P., & Evans, C., <u>The Cambridge History of the Bible</u> Vol. I, pp. 28, 52 - 53, 56 - 57 & Goodspeed, E., <u>The Story of the New Testament</u> pp. 148 - 149 & Weiss, J., <u>Earliest Christianity: A History of the Period A.D. 30 - 150</u> Vol. II, p. 856 & Ethiopian Church, <u>Encyclopedia of Religion</u> Vol. V, p. 174 & Metzger, B., <u>The Early Version of the New Testament</u> p. 101 & Goodspeed, E., <u>A History of Early Christian Literature</u> & Guillamont, A., <u>The Gospel According to Thomas</u> & Griggs, C., <u>Early Egyptian Christianity: From its Origins to 451 C.E.</u> p. 7 & Harnack, A., <u>The Mission and Expansion of Christianity in the first three centuries</u> Vol. II, pp. 159 - 160 & <u>The Lost Books of the Bible and the Forgotten Books of Eden</u> pp. 38 - 59, 82 - 88 - 90 & Higgins, G., <u>Anacalypsis</u> Vol. I, p. 544 & Burkill, T., <u>The Evolution of Christian Thought</u> pp. 25 - 26 & Tompkins, P., <u>The Magic of Obelisks</u> pp. 56 - 57

Africa's Indispensable Role

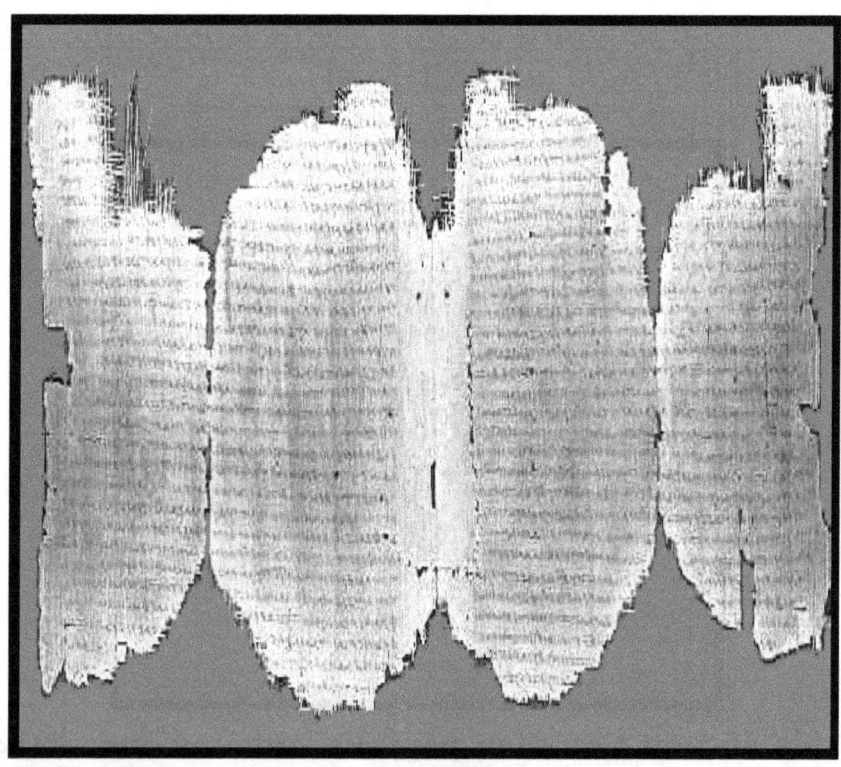

Here is a Coptic Christian papyrus that was discovered in Egypt. Dating back to c.250 CE., it contains passages from the New Testament <u>Book of Luke</u>. Today it is housed in the Chester Beatty Library in Ireland (Gregory-Aland Papyrus 45).

In closing here, Groves steps forward to make the point that the world's oldest surviving <u>Christian manuscripts</u> (i.e., texts written during the 3rd century CE.) were written in the African tongue of the ancient Egyptians! Ackroyd and Evans explain:

<u>"Our earliest Christian manuscripts have much in common. All (with a single exception</u>

Africa & the Written Word

from the third century) come from Egypt; all were found by excavation . . ."[4]

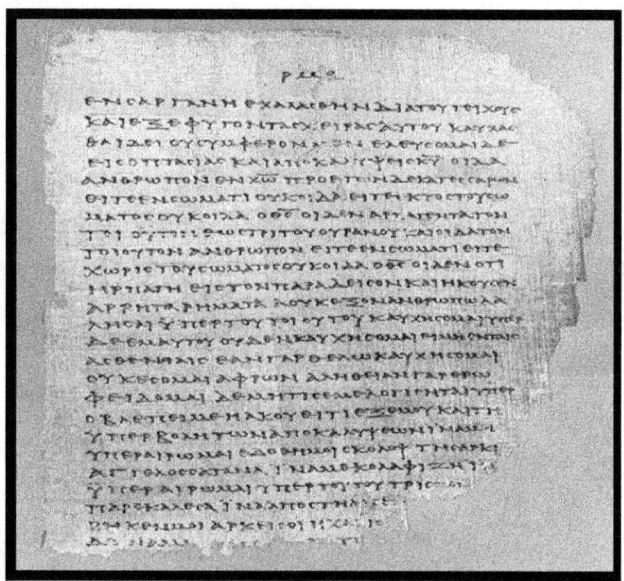

This ancient Christian papyrus contains one of the New Testament epistles of the Apostle Paul (II Corinthians 11:33 – 12:9). Found in Egypt, this Coptic manuscript dates back to c.200 CE. It is also a part of the Chester Beatty Biblical Papyrus Collection (Gregory-Aland Papyrus 46).

---

[4] Ackroyd, P., & Evans, C., The Cambridge History of the Bible Vol. I, pp. 27 - 28, 55 - 56, 62, 601 & Frank, H., Swain, C., & Canby, C., The Bible Through the Ages p. 118 & Budge, E.A., The Dwellers on the Nile p. 187
Here is a rough English translation of the ancient Coptic text Matthew 6: 19 - 21: *"Do not gather for you in treasures upon the earth, the place in which are wont the rust and the moth destroy in it, and the place where are wont the thieves to dig into it to steal. The place wherein thy treasure shall be in it, shall be there thy heart also . . ."*

Pergamos
I know thy works and where thou dwellest

Pergamos

It would be an oversight not to stop and make the point that **_worshipping Christianity during its earliest centuries was no walk in the park! Many Christians were forced to work in mines and rock quarries; while others were tortured, killed by fire, decapitated, and/or eaten alive by wild animals_**. From Carthage to Cyrenaica to Alexandria to Thebes—the early sacrifices and martyrdom of Africa's Christians has been irrefutably established![1] Although many have tried to portray Europeans as the first standard-bearers of the religion—the truth is that the chief religious figures of pagan Rome were early Christianity's greatest persecutors: **_carrying out a campaign of terrorism and murder that ran three centuries_**.[2] Incredibly, Rome killed more than

---

[1] Groves, C., The Planting of Christianity in Africa Vol. I, p. 38 & De Graft-Johnson, J., African Glory p. 40 & Richardson, D., & O'Brien, K., Egypt: A Rough Guide p. 491 & Wellard, J., Lost Worlds of Africa pp. 115 - 116 & Metzger, B., The Early Version of the New Testament p. 104
It is noteworthy that the first recorded Christian Martyr was a North African named, Namphamo. Born in Numidia, the faithful Namphamo is considered to have been of Carthaginian (Canaanite) ancestry. In actual point of fact, scholars have discovered endless lists of martyred Egyptians from the 1st, 2nd, and 3rd centuries.

[2] The Romans supplanted the Ptolemies in Egypt c.30 BCE. This made the Roman Empire the dominant military power in Southern Europe, the Eastern Mediterranean, and North Africa.

Africa's Indispensable Role

three quarters of a million Egyptian Christians in the 3rd century alone! To quote one distinguished theologian: *"The article entitled, La Dictionnaries des dictionnaires states that the Copts who lost their lives in this seventh persecution suffered under Diocletian were eight hundred thousand."*[3]

Though created a millennium before the Christian era, this ancient Phoenician carving captures an occurrence that every Egyptian and Carthaginian Christian would have been all too familiar with: ***The Christians to the Lions!***

---

[3] Misri, I., The Story of the Copts pp. 76 - 77

Pergamos

Briefly, even while the spiritual teachings of the Messiah were revolutionizing North Africa and the Nile Valley—we find the Roman State being vehemently committed to the worship of their traditional gods, the maintenance of their institutions, and the control of their Asian and African provinces. Some of Rome's most popular deities are cited here: Jupiter, Juno, Neptune, Minerva, Venus, Mars, Diana, and Apollo.[4]

Here is a marble bust of a 3rd century CE. Roman flamen. A flamen was a Roman priest who could be assigned to administer over the worship of any one of fifteen major Roman deities. This bust is housed in the Louvre in France.

---

[4] Perowne, S., Roman Mythology & Hyde, W., Paganism to Christianity in the Roman Empire

Africa's Indispensable Role

Atop all of this, mankind's spiritual connection with the Creator was not a principal concern of many of the empire's dignitaries. As a matter fact, Pfeffer would characterize the spiritual ambivalence of the empire's leadership thusly:

> *"By the time of Caesar, the expansion of Rome, with the resulting corruption of the state religion by contact with pagan deities and worships, brought about in Rome an extreme skepticism towards religion. Cicero, himself a member of the sacerdotal order of augurs or official diviners, declared publicly that he did not believe in omens; and Cato said he wondered how two members of the augurs' guild could meet without laughing. Caesar, who was not only head of the secular state but also Pontifex Maximus, [most distinguished Priest] declared in the Senate that he did not believe in a future life . . ."*[5]

Consequently, the malevolent attitude exhibited by Rome towards the Jews and early Christians comes as no real surprise.[6] Yet, with the conversion of

---

[5] Pfeffer, L., Church, State, And Freedom pp. 10 - 11
It is a foregone conclusion that these people were not the progeny of the ancient founders of Etruria.
[6] Pfeffer, L., Church, State, And Freedom pp. 10 - 11 & Robinson, C., Conversion of Europe p. 209 & Griggs, C., Early Egyptian Christianity: From its Origins to 451 C.E. p. 14
The Romans burned Jerusalem to the ground in fighting with the Jews c.70 CE. A great deal of the friction between the

Pergamos

hundreds of thousands of Hebrews and African Gentiles to Christianity (*another autonomous monotheistic religion*) we find that the political hierarchy of Rome was perfectly willing to institute an unprecedented reign of terror against the believers of this new religion.

Murderous animosity would take hold against the Faith by the 1st century reign of Nero. By the beginning of the 2nd century, Trajan pronounced Christians to be "*outlaws*" of a sacrilegious nature. This edict made Christians subject to random execution by such means as being buried alive and/or eaten by ferocious animals. After Trajan's death in 117 CE., a reduction in the number of Christian executions occurred. However, to be a Christian could still be precarious in that the religion's followers were still considered nefarious. Entering the 3rd century, truly concerned about the lack of support by Christians for the emperorship or its pageantry—in 202 CE., Septimius Severus decreed that the existing Christian communities would not be mistreated, so long as they did not convert anyone else to the Faith: *another futile act*.

Romans and Jews was spawned in the Emperor Augustus' decree that dead emperors became a part of the divine pantheon of Rome. Accordingly, anyone who would not worship Caesar was considered to be showing contempt for the state. Eventually, it was decreed that the Jews were allowed to pray for, *but not to*, Caesar. There were more than 4,000,000 Hebrews scattered about the Roman Empire (1,000,000 in Egypt alone).

Africa's Indispensable Role

With all of these measures failing to curb the religion's proliferation, under Decius it was mandated that all property holders had to obtain a certificate that affirmed their devotion to the empire's religious tenets. The Romans made house-to-house searches for these certificates, *which forced many devout African Christians to either abandon their homes*, or be killed. Over and above this, initiating an unparalleled assault against Christianity—Valerian would go so far as to seize Church property, forbid all Christian assemblies, and summarily charge clergymen with high treason! This period of terror and persecution would not be abated until Valerian's death in 260 CE.

But the reprieve was short-lived; in 284 CE., Diocletian did not merely reinstitute Valerian's policies—he began burning churches and the Faith's sacred books. Diocletian also forced the worship of Caesar upon Christian clergymen under the threat of torture (see page xiii). The famous North African theologian Tertullian would say: *"If the Tiber floods to the walls, if the Nile does not flood the fields, if the sky stands still, if the earth shakes, if there is famine, or plague, at once [the public cry instantly goes up]:* **The Christians to the Lions***!"*[7]

---

[7] The American Peoples Encyclopedia Vol. VI, p. 853, Vol. XIV, pp. 464 - 465, Vol. XVIII, p. 967, Vol. XIX, p. 492 & Nero, The World Book Encyclopedia Vol. XII, pp. 5499 - 5500 & Goodspeed, E., A History of Early Christian Literature p. 211 & Pfeffer, L., Church, State, And Freedom

Pergamos

As late as the beginning of the 4th century, Roman law permitted the random persecution of Christians. Actually, this empire was to sponsor the persecution and murder of hundreds of thousands of Christians before public crowds making mock screams of, *"Washed and Saved!"* Indeed, Rome's oppression of Africa's Christians was so malicious that Misri would be moved to observe:

> *"The persecutions that were unleashed against the Christians when Abba Petros became patriarch [Head of the Egyptian Church] were those ordered by Diocletian. They were the fiercest and the longest of all the known persecutions, lasting for over ten years, and not ending till the Patriarch himself was martyred . . . It is impossible to determine the number of Egyptian Christians who lost their lives during Diocletian's persecutions. The tortures and executions*

---

pp. 11 - 13 & Misri, I., The Story of the Copts p. 35 & Wellard, J., Lost Worlds of Africa p. 98 & Mayor, J., & Souter, A., O Septimi Florentis Tertvlliani Apologeticvs: Tertullian's Apology p. 117

Nero was the first Roman politician to use the Christians as a political scapegoat. His ploy was to falsely accuse them of the arson that caused the Great Fire of Rome in 64 CE. Next, Trajan's decree revolved around the fact that the Christians would not worship the Emperor Caesar. Additionally here, the misinterpretation of such scriptural passages as Luke 14:26 and 20:34-35 was also utilized to cast the Faith in a negative light. In passing, the property of Christian martyrs was officially confiscated by the empire. The combined reigns of Decius and Valerian ran from c.249 - 260 CE.

Africa's Indispensable Role

carried on day in day out, and year in, year out, without respite. Tertullian, a priest from Carthage and a contemporary of the times says, 'If martyrs throughout the world were to be put in one side of the scales and the Coptic [Egyptian] martyrs alone were to be put on the other, the latter would outweigh the former.'[8]

EVEN WHILE ROME WOULD RUTHLESSLY MURDER MORE THAN A MILLION EGYPTIAN CHRISTIANS—THE FACT THAT CHRISTIANITY CONTINUED TO THRIVE IN

---

[8] Birley, A., Marcus Aurelius p. 330 & De Graft-Johnson, J., African Glory p. 29, 42 & Misri, I., The Story of the Copts pp. 76 -77 & Angus, S., The Environment of Early Christianity pp. 43 - 44

Here, Angus provides us with a sense of the **blood lust** in the hedonistic empire during the early Christian epoch: "*By a terrible irony her greatest material monument extant is the Colosseum. Rome lost her moral balance in successful campaigns: bloodshed was congenial, and when it ceased abroad she sought it in bloody civil wars . . . they sought excitement and recreation by witnessing in cold blood the agonies of men and animals. Gladiatorial games were introduced in 264 B.C. under the pretext of religion . . . The combatants were slaves, criminals [Christians] or captives; later even freemen entered the arena . . . Exhibitors vied with each other in the numbers exposed to slaughter. Caesar put 320 pair up at once; Agrippa caused 700 pairs to fight in one day . . . under Augustus 10,000 fought . . . Titus . . . put up 3,000; Trajan amused Rome for 123 days by exhibiting 10,000 captives in mutual slaughter . . . Under Titus 5,000 animals perished in a day in the Colosseum . . .*"

Pergamos

AFRICA IS CLEAR TESTAMENT TO THE UNRIVALED FAITH AND DEVOTION OF THE WORLD'S FIRST FOLLOWERS OF THE WAY!

Despite these undeniable findings, there are many who wish to minimize the significance of the religion's early expansion amongst these ancient Black people of the African Continent; however, **principled scholars and theologians cannot**! While Christian institutions, leaders, and a great body of its literature had been enthusiastically embraced throughout Egypt by the 3rd century CE.— the religion was still basically non-existent in Europe! The noted scholar **Adolph von Harnack divulges the fact that before the 4th century, in Western and Upper Italy, the Balkans, Germany, the north and western coast of the Black Sea, Gaul, Belgica, Rhaetia, and Russia—there was no Christianity at all!** On the other hand, the heralded 3rd century chronicler Eusebius would explain—*Christianity abounds in Northeastern Africa!*[9]

---

[9] Robinson, C., Conversion of Europe p. 45 & Harnack, A., The Mission and Expansion of Christianity in the first three centuries Vol. II, pp. 93, 230 - 231, 239 - 240 & Budge, E.A., The Book of the Dead p. 52 & De Ferrari, J., The Fathers of the Church: Eusebius Pamphili-Ecclesiastical History Bks. I - V p. 113 & Eusebius, Grolier Multimedia Encyclopedia
Eusebius (who lived c.260 - 340 CE.) is referred to as the "First Historian" of the Christian Church.

Africa's Indispensable Role

This portrait is of Africa's Saint Mark the Evangelist. It was the Kizhi Monastery in Karelia Russia that commissioned it in the early 1700s. Had it not been for the Apostle Mark's determination, <u>*and the faith of his loyal and courageous 1st century Egyptian followers*</u>, early Christianity might well have failed to survive the inhuman onslaught of the Romans.

Christianity in Ethiopia

Africa's Indispensable Role

Delving into Christianity's historical evolution in Ethiopia, again we discover an early and laudable record. Actually, in light of the ancestral and cultural connections between the Africans of the Northern and Southern Nile—*not to mention the Roman persecution of Christians throughout the Mediterranean for centuries*—it is no surprise that the Faith should begin to take hold in Nubia and Ethiopia well before the Christian conversion of the pantheistic emperors of Rome.

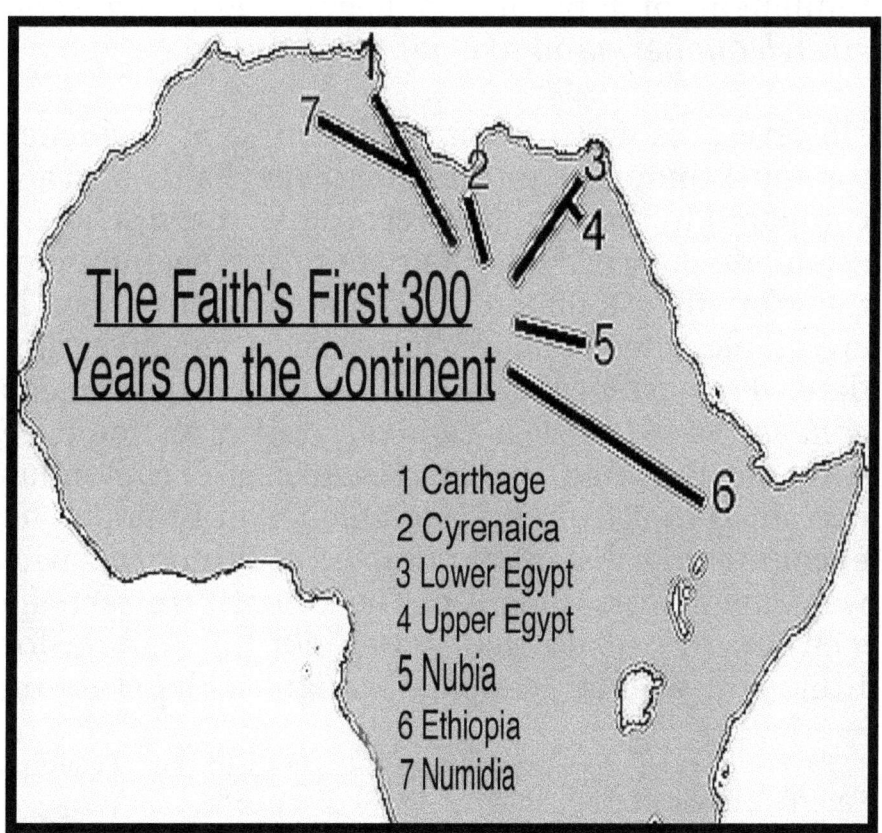

Christianity in Ethiopia

Biblical scripture explains that Philip the Evangelist met and baptized Djan Darada, who was the treasurer of Queen Garsemot IV of Ethiopia, in the 1st century CE. The significance of this is that Djan Darada did not merely become a preacher in his Ethiopian homeland—he would be instrumental in the conversion of his queen to Christianity! Shortly thereafter, Queen Garsemot would construct, and dedicate, a great temple to the Messiah in Ethiopia. In his famous chronicle, Eusebius considers this African queen's 1st century conversion to be the fulfillment of biblical prophecy: *"Ethiopia shall stretch out her hand to God."*[1]

However, insomuch as other documentary evidence for the Ethiopian conversion to the Faith is scant compared to the Egyptian record—Western scholars often cite c.330 CE. as the date of the beginning of the Christian Religion in Ethiopia. But there is creditable anecdotal evidence for a much earlier date. For instance, *even setting Queen Garsemot's conversion aside for a moment*, during an audience with the Egyptian Bishop Athanasius—Frumentius explained that from his adolescence in Ethiopia, he encountered substantial numbers of Ethiopians who were open worshippers of the Christ! In fact, he went on to explain that it was not uncommon for Ethiopian women to wear the sign of the cross on

---

[1] De Ferrari, J., The Fathers of the Church: Eusebius Pamphili-Ecclesiastical History Bks. I - V p. 88
This prophecy was made in Psalms 68: 31.

Africa's Indispensable Role

their foreheads! Despite this information, Western historians routinely point to Frumentius' appointment as Bishop of the Church of Ethiopia by Athanasius of Alexandria in 329 CE., as the state's introduction and acceptance of Christianity.[2]

Here is a Medieval rendering of Ethiopia's Saint Frumentius.

---

[2] Hansberry, L., Pillars in Ethiopian History pp. 69 - 70 & Cox, G., African Empires and Civilizations p. 117 & Windsor, R., From Babylon to Timbuktu pp. 41 - 42 & Misri, I., The Story of the Copts p. 112 & Ethiopian Church Autocephaly, Coptic Encyclopedia Vol. III, p. 980 & Hall, M., The Secret Teachings of All Ages p. CLXXXIII
Hall writes: *"The 'Tau' Cross was the sign which the Lord told the people of Jerusalem to mark upon their foreheads, as related by the Prophet Ezekiel. It was also placed as a symbol of the liberation upon those charged with crimes but acquitted."* In passing, though being raised in Ethiopia, Frumentius appears to have actually been of Phoenician (Canaanite) heritage (see page 33).

Christianity in Ethiopia

This all notwithstanding, Frumentius would return to Ethiopia as the acknowledged head of the kingdom's Church. Upon reaching Ethiopia, Frumentius was well received by Axum's populace and the state's co-regents, King Ezana (Aezanes) and his brother Sayzana (Shaiazana), who were actually old friends of the Southern Nile's newly sanctified Church head!

This is the Obelisk of King Ezana at Axum. Standing 70 feet high, this stone monolith was cut in Ethiopia during the 4th century CE.

Africa's Indispensable Role

Unlike the lands under Roman sway, Frumentius received the full support of his royals. Truth be told, Ezana and Sayzana had publicly professed their acceptance of Christianity well before Frumentius' appointment by Athanasius in Egypt.³ Obviously, this spiritual finding about the heads of Ethiopian society alone—<u>makes it rather imbecilic to assert that the roots of the Faith were not laid in Ethiopia well before the 4th century CE</u>. Indeed, the facts that there was no state persecution of Christians; that many of Ethiopia's Hebrews and Gentiles would have had an affinity for the Faith; and, the early acceptance of the religion by such beloved nobles as Queen Garsemot and Djan Darada, as noted by Eusebius—all totally support the argument for a 2<u>nd</u>, *or even 1<u>st</u>, century conversion claim!*

Nevertheless, soon after Frumentius' official appointment as Abun of Ethiopia, Christianity would hit full bloom along the banks of the Southern Nile. In the words of Hansberry:
> *"As a consequence of the widespread and astonishingly favorable response to*

---

³ Hansberry, L., <u>Pillars in Ethiopian History</u> pp. 70 - 71 & De Graft-Johnson, J., <u>African Glory</u> pp. 81 - 82 & Ethiopian Church, <u>Encyclopedia of Religion</u> Vol. V, pp. 173 – 174 & Ezana, Sayzana, <u>Historical Dictionary of Ethiopia and Eritrea</u> p. 119 & Sayzana, <u>Dictionary of African Biography</u> p. 128
The two brothers may well have been twins. However, it appears that Sayzana was to outlive his brother. The mother of these royals was Queen Sawya.

Christianity in Ethiopia

Frumentius's ministrations, the newly established Ethiopian church was before many months numbering its adherents by the thousands and then by the tens of thousands; and in this great army of converts were recruits representing all levels of Ethiopian society . . ."[4]

In the ensuing decade, the co-regents oversaw the complete conversion of their lands to Christianity. Furthermore, chroniclers explain that there was no retreat from the Faith amongst these co-regents' successors. After the deaths of Ezana and Sayzana, it is explained that the three sons of the latter (Ela Abreha II, Ela Asfeha, and Ela Shahel II) would continue in the holy ways of their predecessors. It so happens that this was no burden, since each of these Ethiopian rulers is recorded as being devoutly

---

[4] Hansberry, L., Pillars in Ethiopian History pp. 72 - 73, 80 & Abun, The Coptic Encyclopedia Vol. I, p. 30 & Doresse, J., Ethiopia p. 62, 82 & Budge, E.A., A History of Ethiopia Vol. I, pp. 3 - 4, 399 - 402 & Misri, I., The Story of the Copts p. 117

The Abun was the highest member of the Ethiopian Church. The older Coptic Christian patriarchs of Egypt ordained many of these Abuns. For example, upon his Egyptian ordination, Frumentius was given the title *Abba Salama,* meaning "Father of Peace." In the years after Frumentius' appointment, we find many Coptic Christian texts being transcribed into an Ethiopian script known as Ge'ez. It must be noted that the Catholic hierarchy of Rome was still trying to undermine the influence of Egypt's patriarchs upon the Ethiopian Church as late as the 17th century CE.

Africa's Indispensable Role

Christian.5 Forasmuch as Axum had long been the most formidable and prosperous kingdom of the Southern Nile at this point in history—it is safe to conclude that by the end of the 4th century, Christianity was firmly rooted throughout the Southern regions of Africa's Nile Valley . . .

A Christian church on the grounds of the Debra Damo Monastery in Ethiopia. Incredibly, this African monastery dates back to the 5th century CE.

---

5 Hansberry, L., Pillars in Ethiopian History pp. 85 – 86
The three sons ruled the nation as co-regents. Interestingly, it is said that the day was divided into three equal parts so that each son might rule a part of each day autonomously. It is noteworthy that their reign is reported has remaining congenial and prosperous throughout.

Christianity in Ethiopia

This photo is of one of the rock-hewn churches built in Lalibela Ethiopia. Known as the Church of Saint George, this building was cut from a single block of stone in the shape of a cross. Ethiopia's King Lalibela built the Church of Saint George in the 13th century CE. This incredible structure is regarded as "One of the Eight Wonders of the World!"

African Martyrs & Standard-Bearers of the Early Faith

African Martyrs & Standard-Bearers

Though having to face centuries of truly ghastly reprisals—hundreds of thousands of North Africans would defy Rome's prohibitions against worshipping Christianity. Even while such defiance could, and often did, necessitate them making the ultimate sacrifice—these Africans refused to yield to the Romans! If the truth is to be told, the beliefs and faith of the body of Christ has seldom, *if ever*, been tested to like degrees. Thus, it is only fitting that we pay tribute to the memory of these courageous African Followers of the Way...

Perpetua

When reflecting upon the early religion's female martyrs, one cannot help but call to mind the brave and devoted Perpetua. She was a 22-year-old Carthaginian woman of noble parentage who committed no crime, other than to devote her life to the worship of Christianity, despite the official decrees of the Romans. Chroniclers explain that she faced her death so courageously that she actually steered the shaking hand of the young centurion who was ordered to murder her.

The incredible zeal that the early African followers had for the Faith is further demonstrated by the fact

Africa's Indispensable Role

that shortly after witnessing Perpetua's murder, her handmaiden Felicitas—*offered up her life to the Romans as well*—so that she could follow her mistress into martyrdom! Witnessing Felicitas' courageous act, ten other Carthaginian Christians from the gathering crowd would spontaneously volunteer to be martyred after her. Thus, on the 17th of July in the city of Carthage, five women and seven men would willingly pay the ultimate price for the love of their Lord.[1]

Bust of an ancient Carthaginian woman

---

[1] De Graft-Johnson, J., African Glory p. 32 & Fremantle, A., A Treasury of Early Christianity p. 216 & O'leary, D., The Saints of Egypt p. 14
Perpetua had a young child at the time of her martyrdom and Felicitas was eight months pregnant. Different writers have placed the year of their martyrdom between 180 and 203 CE.

African Martyrs & Standard-Bearers

Tertullian

An historian of the Faith remarked: *"Tertullian . . . attacked the enemies of the church, particularly the Roman government, who persecuted the first Christian communities, and he wrote with an eloquence and zest which was totally African."*[2] Quintus Tertullian was born in the North African city of Carthage c.160 CE. As the son of a military man, Tertullian's youth was spent worshipping the traditional gods of Carthage: Tanit, Baal Ammon, and so forth. However, during his teen years, he began to be disturbed by the plight of the Christians; but as he was from a well-to-do family, most of his days were occupied with teachers, friends, and servants who insulated him from the predicaments of the Christians.[3]

By adulthood, Tertullian was so well educated and traveled that he was proficient in several languages. But despite all of his early worldliness, he would

---

[2] Ennabli, A., & Slim, H., <u>Carthage: A Visit to the Ruins</u> p. 16
[3] Goodspeed, E., <u>A History of Early Christian Literature</u> p. 211 & De Graft-Johnson, J., <u>African Glory</u> p. 41 & Fremantle, A., <u>A Treasury of Early Christianity</u> p. 216
It's said that the impetus for Tertullian's conversion to Christianity, was witnessing the courage of Perpetua and the eleven others who were martyred with her.

Africa's Indispensable Role

find himself being drawn to Christianity like a moth to the flame. He was probably in his early to mid-twenties when he openly accepted the Faith. As a passionate defender of the religion, he would soon begin to publicly criticize Rome and the believers of the Gnostic Religion: many Gnostic Christian sects rising up in Egypt during this period.[4] It is also important to note that it was this African who was the first theologian to translate Christian scripture into Latin! You see, *on the off chance that a Roman actually felt the need to read Christian scripture*—the general populace of Rome could not prior to the 3rd century CE. because of the language barrier.[5]

---

[4] Hall, M., The Secret Teachings of All Ages pp. XXV - XXVI & Crombie, F., The Writings of Origen pp. 403 - 404 & The Gnostic Scriptures p. 206, 420
Contrary to Tertullian and Origen's views, some sects were teaching that Judeo-Christianity was an esoteric religion with secrets that were only to be taught to an initiated class. As a matter of fact, Tertullian felt that the Gnostics deviated from the actual teachings to such an extent, they placed greater emphasis on secret greetings and self-knowledge than the worship of God. Remarkably, the Gnostics did not even believe that the Messiah was crucified! Believing that Christ could not die—the Gnostic view was that an African named Simon was miraculously substituted for Christ on the cross at the time of the crucifixion. In passing, many Gnostic texts have come down to us in their original Egyptian script.

[5] De Graft-Johnson, J., African Glory p. 41 & Goodspeed, E., A History of Early Christian Literature p. 210 & Ackroyd, P., & Evans, C., The Cambridge History of the Bible Vol. I, p. 345 & Robinson, C., Conversion of Europe p. 210 & Higgins, G., Anacalypsis Vol. I, pp. 458 - 459, 461, Vol. II, p. 20

African Martyrs & Standard-Bearers

As a dynamic and influential advocate of a strong Church, Tertullian is accredited with making the following contributions to the early Christian Religion:[6]

The use of the term *Trinity* in Christian philosophy.

Advocating the separation between Christians and all of the affairs of the Roman State.

Stressing moral discipline and restraint for Christians.

Incidentally, the Fathers of the early Church opposed the vocation of acting. In fact, Tertullian would go so far as to proclaim Rome's chariot races,

---

As an accomplished linguist, Tertullian translated many works into Greek and Latin. In passing, language would not have been a tremendous obstacle for many North African Christians; indeed, Godfrey Higgins considered the ancient Chaldean, Hebrew, Phoenician, and Egyptian languages—all to be a part of the same linguistic family (see page 122).

[6] Burkill, T., The Evolution of Christian Thought pp. 58 - 59 & Mayor, J., & Souter, A., O Septimi Florentis Tertvlliani Apologeticvs: Tertullian's Apology & Goodspeed, E., A History of Early Christian Literature p. 211 & King, A., Quotations in Black p. 7 & Fremantle, A., A Treasury of Early Christianity p. 59

Possessing one of the finest intellects in the early Christian realm, Tertullian did not merely warn Christians against failing to understand what is—*but groveling in something that never was* . . .

Africa's Indispensable Role

gladiator contests, public gatherings, and theatrical events—all to be the work of the Devil.

This son of Carthage also explained: *"Men remain in ignorance as long as they hate, and they hate unjustly, as long as they remain in ignorance!"*

While Tertullian authored more than two-dozen works, the saying that this African theologian is probably best known for is the declaration: *"The Blood of the Martyrs is the seed of the Church."*

Ruins of ancient Carthage with the Mediterranean Sea in the background.

African Martyrs & Standard-Bearers

The Bishop Cyprian

The heralded Bishop Cyprian of Carthage lived during the 3rd century CE. As a member of a well-established Carthaginian family, it is explained that Cyprian did not accept Christianity until adulthood.[7] This aside, it was so clear that Cyprian was filled with the Holy Spirit that his diocesan rise only took two years! As Bishop, Cyprian stressed baptizing the young and believed that the Church should be founded upon the teachings of the Apostle Peter. This North African Bishop was also celebrated for giving a great deal of his personal wealth to the poor!

Guiding the Church of Carthage during a period of increased persecution by the Romans, Cyprian was forced to spend much of his tenure in hiding and exile. Eventually, the Romans captured and murdered him c.258 CE. However, the courage and character of this African Saint was truly commendable. An ancient historian has left us this incredible account of Cyprian's martyrdom:

---

[7] Smith, W., <u>Dictionary of Greek and Roman Mythology</u> Vol. I, pp. 912 - 916 & Fremantle, A., <u>A Treasury of Early Christianity</u> p. 229 & De Graft-Johnson, J., <u>African Glory</u> pp. 41 - 42
Cyprian walked away from a successful law practice and became a Christian c.245 CE.

Africa's Indispensable Role

"On the morrow, being September 14, a great crowd gathered in the morning to the House of Sextus in accordance with the command of Galerius Maximus the Proconsul. And so the same Galerius the Proconsul ordered that Cyprian the Bishop should be brought before him on the morrow where he sat in the Hall Sauciolum. When he had been brought before him, Galerius Maximus the Proconsul said to Cyprian the Bishop: 'Are you Thascius Cyprianus?'
Cyprian the Bishop answered: 'I am.'
Galerius Maximus the Proconsul said: 'Have you taken on your self to be Pope of persons holding to sacrilegious opinions?'
Cyprian the Bishop answered: 'Yes.'
Galerius Maximus the Proconsul said: 'The most sacred Emperors have commanded you to perform the rite.'
Cyprian the Bishop answered: 'I refuse.'
Galerius the Proconsul said: 'Consider your own interest.'
Cyprian the Bishop answered: 'Do as you are bid. In so clear a case there is no need for consideration.'
Galerius Maximus, having conferred with the Council, gave sentence hardly and reluctantly in these terms: 'You have long lived in the holding of sacrilegious opinions, and have joined with your self very many members of an abominable conspiracy, and have set your

African Martyrs & Standard-Bearers

self up as an enemy of the Gods of Rome and the religious ordinances, nor have the pious and most sacred Emperors Valerian and Gallienus ... and the most noble Caesar, been able to recall you to the observance of their rites. And since therefore you have been convicted as the contriver and the standard-bearer in most atrocious crimes, you shall be an example to those whom by your wickedness you have joined with you: Discipline shall be vindicated in your blood.' With these words he read from his tablets the sentence: 'It is our pleasure that Thascius Cyprianus should be executed by the sword.' Cyprian the Bishop proclaimed: 'Thanks be to God!'"[8]

---

[8] Fremantle, A., A Treasury of Early Christianity pp. 229 - 232 & Marshall, T., The Glorious Martyrdom of St. Cyprian & The Lost Books of the Bible and The Forgotten Books of Eden pp. 177, 187 - 196 & Malcioln, J., The African Origins of Modern Judaism pp. 125 - 126 & Radice, B., Letters, and Penegyricus Vol. II, pp. 287 - 293

Unfortunately, as the Romans had a long history of murdering Jews and Christians, such ancient testimony is not that unusual. For instance, an incredible account in The Fourth Book of Maccabees canonizes the seven sons of a Hebrew woman—*who all chose to be brutally tortured and murdered by a Roman tyrant*—rather than watch their mother be forced to eat pork! To illustrate the barbarism that the Hebrews faced, more than 3,600 (men, women, and children) were indiscriminately killed during the last two years of Nero's reign alone.

Africa's Indispensable Role

Directing his friends in the crowd to give his executioner twenty-five pieces of gold upon his death—the North African Bishop Thascius Caecilius Cyprianus bowed in prayer and was executed on the 14th day of September in 258 CE. (see page 22). Down through the ages, Cyprian has been commemorated for this profound ancient utterance:

"Every age is reminded by what it hears, that what has been done can be done again. Transgressions never die from the passage of age; crime is never erased by time; vice is never buried in oblivion."[9]

Artistic rendering of Africa's Bishop Cyprian

---

[9] King, A., Quotations in Black p. 8
Cyprian made this remark c.246 CE.

African Martyrs & Standard-Bearers

Origen

Examining the writings of the African heads of the world's early Church, Origen's pen leaps to the fore! Known as the Christian World's "First Great Theologian," Origen is said to have authored hundreds of splendid Christian works.[10] In his De Principiis, Origen writes:

> "The logos became flesh in order to aid man in the recovery of his pristine state of unblemished communion with God. The Holy Spirit also promotes salvation by inspiring men to holiness of life!"[11]

A son of Egyptian Christians, it is interesting that the name *Origen* actually means, "Son of Horus." Born c.185 CE., Origen was the eldest of nine children. His father Leonidas was martyred for the Faith c.202 CE. Attending the Catechetical Institute during Clement's tenure, the young Origen would become a devout Christian. Exhibiting a strong character and brilliant intellect, he was given the name *Adamantius*, because of his unwavering commitment to the ascetic lifestyle. Origen's faith and insight was so remarkable that Demetrius chose

---

[10] Trigg, J., Origen p. 1 & Fremantle, A., A Treasury of Early Christianity p. 66 & Misri, I., The Story of the Copts p. 38

[11] Burkill, T., The Evolution of Christian Thought pp. 70 – 71

Africa's Indispensable Role

him to head the Catechetical Institute in 215 CE. Origen would instruct his pupils as follows:

> *"Behave like the sculptor of a statue; he carves, he scrapes, he polishes until he produces something beautiful. Like unto the sculptor, do not cease from shaping your own self until the divine radiance glows within you."*[12]

Origen would face two decades of great controversy and tremendous hardship after his appointment in Alexandria. Yet, he remained steadfast in his stance against Rome. For example, inasmuch as the world's first Christians were <u>martyrs</u> not <u>murderers</u>—it is to be noted that Origen and Tertullian openly denounced the service of Christians in the Roman military![13] He also taught that <u>it is better to be wise—than to seem wise</u>. Origen was captured, tortured, and martyred at Tyre c.250 CE. Truly, a man of his convictions, Origen would declare:

---

[12] Catechetical School of Alexandria, <u>The Coptic Encyclopedia</u> Vol. II, pp. 470 - 471 & Misri, I., <u>The Story of the Copts</u> pp. 23 - 25, 34 - 35, 39 & Fremantle, A., <u>A Treasury of Early Christianity</u> p. 66 & Burghardt, W., Lawler, T., & Dillion, J., <u>Ancient Christian Writers: The Works of the Fathers in Translation</u> Vol. 54, pp. 2 - 3 & De Graft-Johnson, J., <u>African Glory</u> p. 39 & Trigg, J., <u>Origen</u> p. 10
Origen's mother may well have been a Jewish convert to Christianity.
[13] Robinson, C., <u>Conversion of Europe</u> p. 208 & I John 2: 21
A fitting stance for so much as, *"no lie is of the truth!"*

African Martyrs & Standard-Bearers

"I want to be a Man of the Church. I do not want to be called by the name of some founder of a heresy, but by the name of Christ, and to bear that name which is blessed on the earth. It is my desire, in deed as in spirit, both to be and be called, a Christian!"[14]

Spanish portrayal of Mary and the Christ child. It was painted by Riccia in the 17th century.

Even while many of Origen's writings have not been recovered, he is heralded for his commentaries on

---

[14] King, A., Quotations in Black p. 8 & Origen, Grolier Multimedia Encyclopedia & Von Balthasar, H., Origen: Spirit and Fire p. frontispiece

Africa's Indispensable Role

most of the books of the Bible. Furthermore, Origen's <u>Hexapla</u> has been celebrated down through the ages. Clearly, Origen was a fervent and tireless communicant of the Gospels. Amazingly, while St. Jerome places the number of Origen's writings at about 800—St. Epiphanius places the number closer to six thousand![15] Let me leave you with this quote by Misri about this brilliant African theologian:

> *"Origen is the enigma of ecclesiastical history. He was a genius in every since of the word: a prolific writer, great teacher, an ardent doer. His bold admirers and devoted followers were innumerable, and yet he did not escape having strong adversaries who tried to malign him. His name stirred the most enthusiastic devotion and the most passionate antagonism. Such a singular destiny could only heighten the attraction of the singularly interesting figure of ancient Christianity."*[16]

---

[15] Goodspeed, E., <u>A History of Early Christian Literature</u> pp. 242 - 245 & Trigg, J., <u>Origen</u> p. 1 & Fremantle, A., <u>A Treasury of Early Christianity</u> p. 66 & Misri, I., <u>The Story of the Copts</u> p. 38

Considered one of the most ambitious Christian works ever endeavored by one person, Origen's <u>Hexapla</u> is a compilation of six versions of the Old Testament scored side by side for study! St. Jerome was probably the most famous student of Origen's <u>Hexapla</u>.

[16] Misri, I., <u>The Story of the Copts</u> p. 34 & Fremantle, A., <u>A Treasury of Early Christianity</u> pp. 66 - 69 & Higgins, G., <u>Anacalypsis</u> Vol. I, p. 85

African Martyrs & Standard-Bearers

Antony

One other distinguished Egyptian of the early Church was Saint Antony. Widely held in the Old World as the "Father of Monks and a Healer of Men"—this celebrated African has been accredited with founding the Christian eremitic and ascetic ways of living. Antony was born to a well-to-do Egyptian family c.251 CE. Being devout Christians, Antony's parents saw to it that their son was

---

Origen was also a vocal proponent of astrology. In commemoration of his lifelong friend and teacher, Gregory Thaumaturus shared a letter from Origen which states the following: *"All hail to thee in God, most excellent and reverend sir, son Gregory, from Origen . . . my desire for you has been that you should direct the whole force of your intelligence to Christianity as your end . . . And I wish that you should take with you on the one hand those parts of the philosophy of the Greeks which are fit, as it were, to serve as general or preparatory studies for Christianity, and on the other hand so much Geometry and Astronomy as may be helpful for the interpretation of the Holy Scriptures . . ."* He continues: *"Do you then, sir, my son, study first of all the divine Scriptures. Study them, I say! For we require to study the divine writings deeply, lest we should speak of them faster than we think; and while you study these divine works with a believing and God-pleasing intention, knock . . . And do not become content with knocking and seeking, for what is most necessary for understanding divine things is prayer, and in urging us to this the savior says not only, Knock, and it shall be opened to you, and Seek, and ye shall find, but also Ask, and it shall be given you!"* (see page xi)

Africa's Indispensable Role

educated in the ways of the Faith from an early age. Although a quiet and shy child, Antony is purported to never have been more uninhibited than when attending church. Shortly after turning twenty, Antony's parents bestowed a fine inheritance upon him. However, six months later Antony sold his estate and gave the proceeds to the poor!

Making a commitment to the eremitic way, Antony lived as a recluse—fasting and praying for several years. During this period, Antony is said to have faced, *and overcome*, several difficult trials of the Devil. With this, it is said that he became a spirit-filled person capable of healing and performing great miracles! As he was to have a profound influence on all of the Christians who came into contact with him—many Egyptians wanted to follow the eremitic path of Saint Antony. Thus, he would establish a community of monks at Pispir (modern Der el Memun) Egypt.

Twenty years later, Antony desired an even greater hermitage. He went further into the African desert near the foot of Mount Qulzum. Sustaining himself through gardening and the gifts of visiting monks, Antony spent the next 40 years in relative seclusion, except for two occasions when he went to Alexandria, to help Bishop Athanasius repudiate the doctrine of Arius. As a committed ascetic to the very end, Antony died a natural death at Mount Qulzum c.356 CE. Today, a Christian Monastery

African Martyrs & Standard-Bearers

known as Dayr Anba Antoniyos stands at Mount Qulzum in commemoration of this wonderful Egyptian Saint![17]

This is the Monastery of Saint Antony in the Eastern Desert of Egypt. Dating back to the 4th century CE., this monastery is one of Coptic Egypt's most respected institutions!

---

[17] De Graft-Johnson, J., African Glory pp. 39 - 40 & Fremantle, A., A Treasury of Early Christianity pp. 475 - 477, 481 & Farmer, D., Oxford Dictionary of Saints pp. 19 - 20 & Antony of Egypt, Saint, The Coptic Encyclopedia Vol. I, pp. 149 - 150
As one of the most influential clergymen of the 4th century CE., Christians throughout Egypt and Palestine followed the precepts of Saint Antony.

Africa's Indispensable Role

Victoria

Another brave African woman to make the supreme sacrifice for the religion was Victoria of Carthage. Daring to openly practice the Faith during the reign of Diocletian—Victoria was apprehended, questioned, and tortured to death c.304 CE. Eyewitnesses tell us that even in the face of barbarous cruelty, Victoria was to display an exemplary character. As a matter of fact, commanders of the Roman Empire are actually said to have used accounts of the bravery of martyrs like Victoria to embolden their troops when facing difficult odds on the battlefield.[18]

Pacome

Before we get to the life of Pacome, I need to explain that while monastic living was an old concept to Egyptian spiritualists, ancient chroniclers tell us that it was an Egyptian known as Ammun, who established the first Christian monastic community c.315 CE. This was centuries before any such settlement was established in

---

[18] Davies, J., Daily Life of Early Christians pp. 76 - 80

Europe. Ammun's monastery was located in the delta at the Mount of Nitria.[19] Yet, as for the subject matter at hand, the Egyptian Monk Pacome (Pachomius) is considered to be the first Christian to establish monastic communals for both sexes—a concept that would spread throughout Egypt and the Old World![20]

Born c.292 CE., Pacome was the son of non-Christian Egyptians of the highlands. While serving in the Roman military as a young man, the charity and devotion of the Christians he encountered in the Nile Valley would have a profound affect on him. Eventually, Pacome converted to Christianity and became a disciple of the Egyptian ascetic Palamon. After several years of study and prayerful meditation in the company of Palamon, two facts became exceedingly clear to Pacome: first, <u>true Christians cannot attain peace and joy as long as they are immersed in the folly of ungodly nations</u>; and second, with the great expansion of the Faith amongst both sexes, the eremitic lifestyle could, *over the course of time*, prove counter-productive.

The first monastery of Pacome was founded on the Island of Tabennisi in the Egyptian highlands near

---

[19] Monasticism, <u>Encyclopedia of Early Christianity</u> p. 615
[20] Pachomius, <u>The Coptic Encyclopedia</u> Vol. VI, pp. 1859 - 1860
In passing, Christian monasteries would not find their way to Europe until the end of Pacome's life (see page xiv).

Africa's Indispensable Role

Thebes. The monks of Pacome's *koinonia* (community) were divided into 24 classes. The koinonia supported themselves through shipbuilding, agriculture, and basket making. The proceeds were placed in a communal treasury and distributed according to need. To provide you with some idea of the Christian devotion and dedication of Pacome—before his death in 346 CE., he had founded nine monasteries and two convents. This was a remarkable achievement inasmuch as Pacome would initiate some 5,000 Africans into the Christian koinonia lifestyle! According to Ferguson:

> *"The sources are replete with evidence for the widespread existence of monks and monasteries up and down the Nile Valley. A party of travelers who visited the monasteries of Egypt in 394 reported in their* **Historia Monachorum** *the seemingly endless number of monastic establishments of varied type between Lycopolis (Assuit) and Alexandria. In the town of Oxyrhynchus, they noted that 'the city is so full of monasteries that the very walls resound with the voices of monks . . .'"*[21]

---

[21] Pachomius, Oxford Dictionary of Saints pp. 309 - 310 & Monasticism, Encyclopedia of Early Christianity pp. 615 - 618 & Pachomius, The Coptic Encyclopedia Vol. VI, pp. 1859 - 1860 & Robinson, C., Conversion of Europe p. 9 & Doresse, J., Ethiopia p. 64 & Boak, A., & Sinnigen, W., A History of Rome to A.D. 565 p. 510 & Acts of Paul & Thecla & Lloyd, S., Early Highland Peoples of Anatolia pp. 84, 124 - 135

African Martyrs & Standard-Bearers

Here is an 11th century Russian fresco of the beautiful and brave Saint Thecla. Egypt's Coptic manuscripts explain that she was one of the first virgins to whole-heartedly embrace the eremitic lifestyle and take the Christian vow of celibacy! She was a devout acetic for seventy-two years.

By 356 CE., Oxyrhynchus is reported to have had 10,000 monks and 20,000 consecrated virgins! Saint Pacome is also believed to have charged the Abba Yohannes with going to Ethiopia to spread the gospel and the koinonia way (see page 49). Even while Athanasius took Egyptian monks from Egypt to Rome in 341 CE., the organizing of monasteries in Western Europe did not begin until the 6th century CE., under the direction of Benedict. Finally, Saint Thecla, who was honored by Africa's monks, was of Phrygian (Canaanite) ancestry.

Africa's Indispensable Role

The Pa-Pas

It should also be explained that Africans would play a role in the early papacy of Rome. Actually, the first African Pope was Victor I who took office c.189 CE. For accuracy's sake, let me reiterate that during the era of Victor I the Church of Rome was hardly the influential body it would later become. Melchiades was Rome's second Black Pope. He served during the era of the Roman State's conversion to Christianity. And Gelasius was the third Black Pope. He held the office from 492 to 496 CE. (*For so much as many Blacks inhabited the Roman Empire before, and during, the rise of Christianity in Europe—we needn't be shocked that there were Black popes. In actual point of fact, the Roman Empire even had Black emperors.*)

It is noteworthy that the name *Pa-Pa,* was a designation for the Roman deity, Jupiter (☠). Furthermore, the papal term *Pontiff,* is derived from Rome's high priestly pagan title, "Pontifex Maximus" (see pages 35, 91, and 98). Yet, as for the actual office—*juxtaposed with later centuries*—the early pa-pas (popes) served much more like bishops. As for the religious status of the office today, let me simply defer to Higgins: "*The Canonists maintain that the Pope is not subject to human law; that he cannot be judged either by the Emperor or by the clergy collectively, neither by kings nor by the people; that it is necessary to salvation to believe, that all creatures are subject to him . . ."*[22]

Papal Insignia

---

[22] Diggs, E., Black Chronology pp. 11 - 12 & Pope, The World Book Encyclopedia Vol. XV, p. 666 & Boak, A., & Sinnigen, W., A History of Rome to A.D. 565 p. 504 & Robinson, C., Conversion of Europe pp. 211 - 212 & Rogers, J.A., Sex and Race Vol. I, p. 86 & Hodgson, M., The Venture of Islam: Conscience and History in a World Civilization Vol. I, p. 139 & Birley, A., Septimius Severus: The African Emperor & Higgins, G., Anacalypsis Vol. II, p. 52, 54

Academicians agree that while there is some evidence of Christianity in Italy (Rome and Puteoli) by the end of the 1st century—there is **absolutely nothing** to suggest that these communities were as large, dynamic, or influential as those of North Africa! Truth be told, the Christians of Italy did not even begin to recognize the spiritual authority of the bishops of Rome until the 4th century CE. Over and above that, as late as the 5th century (well after Constantine's edict calling for the empire's conversion to the Faith) the Italian poet Severus Sanctus Endelechius would write: *"Sisnum quod perhibent esse crucis Dei, Magnis qui colitur solus in urbibus"* (*"Christians can only be found in the large towns"*).

Africa's Indispensable Role

Arius

Having determined that Africans were to play a crucial role in the establishment of early Christianity—it would be an oversight to portray the African Church as developing without any internal discord. For example, Arius was born in North Africa during the 3rd century CE. Though reared and educated at Alexandria, in 318 CE., Arius would introduce a controversial doctrine concerning the trinity and the origin of the Messiah. **Arius' view tended to cast the Christ as a prophet, which denied him any divinity with the Supreme and most Holy God**! These beliefs were roundly denounced, and a council of one hundred North African bishops would excommunicate him by a vote of 98 to 2 in Alexandria c.321 CE. But the controversy over Arius' doctrine did not die there; it lingered in segments of the Church for another four years.

In 325 CE., the Council of Nicea was convened to settle the matter once and for all. To demonstrate just how non-European Christianity's hierarchy was during the 4th century—of the 318 clergymen called to this assembly—all but 6 were from North Africa and Western Asia. This assembly would not merely condemn Arius' teachings, but banish him to Illyria (modern Albania)! In addition, the officials of the council determined that it would be prudent to take one more step. In the hope of heading off any more contentious doctrines—it was decided that they should develop a short declaration that outlined the basic beliefs of the Church. Today the body's declaration is known as the Nicene Creed.

I believe in one God the Father Almighty, Maker of heaven and earth. And of all things visible and invisible:
And in one Lord Jesus Christ, the only-begotten Son of God, Begotten of his Father before all worlds, God of God, Light of Light, Very God of very God, Begotten, not made, Being of one substance with the Father, By whom all things were made: Who for us men and for our salvation came down from heaven, And was made incarnate by the Holy Ghost of the Virgin Mary, And was made man, And was crucified also for us under Pontius Pilate. He suffered and was buried, And the third day he rose again according to the Scriptures, And ascended into heaven. And sitteth on the right hand of the Father. And he shall come again with glory to judge both the quick and the dead: Whose kingdom shall have no end.

And I believe in the Holy Ghost, The Lord and giver of life, Who proceedeth from the Father (and the Son), Who with the Father and the Son together is worshipped and glorified, who spake by the Prophets. And I believe in one Catholick and Apostolick Church. I acknowledge one Baptism for

Africa's Indispensable Role

the remission of sins. And I look for the resurrection of the dead, And the Life of the world to come. Amen.

The Nicene Creed was written by two Egyptians and a Caesarean: Alexandros, 19th Patriarch of the Church of Alexandria; Athanasius, his deacon; and Leontius, Bishop of Caesarea of Cappadocia (Western Asia). Although Arius died c.336 CE., many Goths are said to have been in acceptance of his doctrine as late as the 6th century CE.[23]

---

[23] Smith, W., Dictionary of Greek and Roman Mythology Vol. I, pp. 345 - 347 & De Graft-Johnson, J., African Glory pp. 46 - 47 & Misri, I., The Story of the Copts pp. 97 - 98, 102 - 105, 563 & Arius, Universal Standard Encyclopedia Vol. II, p. 383 & Arius and Arianism, Encyclopedia of Philosophy pp. 162 - 164 & Hansberry, L., Pillars in Ethiopian History pp. 86 - 87, 95 - 96 & Robinson, C., The Conversion of Europe p. 173 & Donatism, Encyclopedia of Religion pp. 420 - 421 & Griggs, C., Early Egyptian Christianity: From its Origins to 451 C.E. p. 99

A bit earlier in the century, another bitter Church dispute took place—it was known as the Donatist Controversy. In short, the North African Church was split over the decision of Constantine to permit Caecilian to lead the Church of Carthage in 311 CE. The essential point of contention was that Caecilian and Felix of Apthungi (one of his followers) acquiesced to Roman pressure during the era of Christian persecution under Diocletian (c.303 - 305 CE.). In fact, their conduct was seen as so egregious that many Christians considered them traitors to the Faith! With such a long history of martyrdom in North Africa, many Christians could not stomach the appointment of Caecilian and immediately denounced him. However, as Constantine supported

African Martyrs & Standard-Bearers

This is a depiction of Saint Athanasius of Alexandria. Painted in the 1600s by an unknown European artist, this Christian icon is kept in the Varna Archeological Museum in Varna Bulgaria.

Caecilian, he would officially retain the position. Eventually, a group led by Donatus of Casae Nigrae took up the opposition's cause. The net effect of this was a serious schism in the Carthaginian Church that would not ultimately be resolved for 200 years.

Africa's Indispensable Role

Augustine

No discussion of the early Church could be complete without some acknowledgment of the North African Bishop Saint Augustine! Aurelius Augustinus was born in Tagaste of the North African state of Numidia in 357 CE. His mother was a Christian woman named Monica; interestingly, his father Patricius was not a believer. Nevertheless, wanting the best for their son, Augustine's parents saw to it that he was educated in Carthage.

As a student, Augustine became proficient in grammar and rhetoric. Traveling throughout the Mediterranean as a young man, Augustine is also reported to have actually spent some time teaching in Milan Italy. After mastering the philosophies of several theorists, particularly the 2nd century Persian, Mani, Augustine decided to wholeheartedly embrace the Christian Religion; his baptism took place in 387 CE. Returning to Africa shortly thereafter, he would become a priest c.391 CE. Augustine displayed such brilliance in the pulpit that he was appointed Bishop of Hippo in 396 CE. By this time, Rome had ended its vigorous persecution of Christians, which made the bishop's choice to live in a monastery legal in the sight of the empire—*though unpopular with his friends* . . .

African Martyrs & Standard-Bearers

But domicile aside, the new Bishop of Hippo would soon become a thorn in the side of the Roman State!<u>24</u> Through the decades, Augustine was unfailing in establishing Christian parameters that opposed all forms of Roman hypocrisy. For instance, in his <u>City of God</u> this African Saint chastised the Romans for such indiscretions as attempting to increase their empire through war, their treatment of early Christians, and their shameful public vice.<u>25</u> Actually, the Saint's attitude towards Rome can be best ascertained through this passage found in De Graft-Johnson's <u>African Glory</u>: *"Augustine asserts that unless a State is a community for ethical purposes and unless it is held together by strong moral ties, it is nothing except 'highway robbery on a large scale.'"*[26]

---

[24] De Graft-Johnson, J., <u>African Glory</u> pp. 16, 42 - 46 & Rogers, J.A., <u>Sex and Race</u> Vol. I, pp. 88 - 89 & Manichaeism, <u>Encyclopedia of Philosophy</u> Vol. V, pp. 149 - 150 & Bowder, D., <u>Who was Who in the Roman World</u> p. 132 & Augustine of Hippo, <u>Oxford Dictionary of Saints</u> pp. 25 - 26 & Augustine, <u>Universal Standard Encyclopedia</u> Vol. II, p. 519

The ancient city of Hippo (Hippone) is modern day Annaba Algeria. Manichaeism was a philosophy of concordant dualism. Through his spiritual mind, the Manichaean was charged with discerning the good in the material world, while rejecting evil. Some of the religion's patriarchs were Adam, Jesus, and Mani. While a Manichaean, Augustine lived with a mistress for 15 years. The couple had a son whose name was Adeodatus.

[25] Oates, W., <u>Basic Writings of Saint Augustine</u>
[26] De Graft-Johnson, J., <u>African Glory</u> p. 46

Africa's Indispensable Role

This dynamic painting is of North Africa's Saint Augustine of Carthage. Created by the Italian artist Simone Sanese in the 1300s, it is a wonderful depiction of the illustrious Church Father!

African Martyrs & Standard-Bearers

Through the ages Christian historians have marveled over this African's genius. He is considered to have been the most influential Christian figure since the Apostle Paul! It should be noted that Augustine was also the Pope of the 44 bishops of the Third Council of Carthage.[27]

Some of this prolific theologian's most heralded works are <u>City of God</u>, <u>Confessions</u>, and <u>De Trinitate</u>. Contemporary scholars explain:

> *"In his great apologetic work, the **City of God**, Augustine appeared in the role of seer, unfolding the meaning of the past and the secrets of the future with abundant learning and fertility of imagination. Ten of the twenty-two books into which this long work is divided are devoted to refuting the pagan notion that the worship of the gods insures prosperity in this life or in the life to come. The remaining twelve books trace the origin, progress, and destiny of the two cities—one of God, the other of this world—with the final triumph of the former, which is the Christian*

---

[27] Augustine of Hippo, <u>Oxford Dictionary of Saints</u> pp. 25 - 26 & <u>The Lost Books of the Bible and The Forgotten Books of Eden</u> p. 293 & Hefele, C., <u>Canons of the Council of Carthage May 1 418</u>
In 418 CE., the Council of Carthage determined that the Pelagian doctrines of human nature, original sin, and grace should be denounced and replaced by doctrines that were developed and advanced by Augustine.

Africa's Indispensable Role

Church. His other works include the famous autobiography **Confessions** *(397), which is widely read, even today. St. Augustine is invoked as the patron of theologians, printers, and brewers . . ."*[28]

One might deem it ironic that after admonishing the Romans for more than three decades, Augustine would die of a virus that he contracted in Carthage during the invasion of the Vandals in 430 CE. However, today, Augustine is universally considered to have been one of the early "<u>Doctors of the Christian Church</u>." Allow me to close with this proclamation by Kristeller, about the African Saint who has come to be known as, Augustine of Hippo: "*We may characterize him as the greatest theologian and philosopher among Latin Christians, and perhaps the greatest Latin thinker of antiquity . . .*"[29]

---

[28] Augustine, <u>Universal Standard Encyclopedia</u> Vol. II, p. 519

[29] De Graft-Johnson, J., <u>African Glory</u> p. 54 & Smith, W., <u>Dictionary of Greek and Roman Biography and Mythology</u> Vol. III, pp. 962 - 963 & Kristeller, P., <u>Renaissance Though and Its Sources</u> p. 226

In Kristeller's remark here, "*Latin Christians*" simply means—Christians of the early Church who lived in a province of the Roman Empire. Parenthetically, one other great North African theologian of the 5th century was the Cyrenaean Synesius. Tracing his ancestry back to the Dorian Ruler Eurysthenes, Synesius' eclectic pen has proven to be an inspiration to ancient and modern Christians alike!

Constantine
& Christianity
in Europe

Africa's Indispensable Role

Leaving the early centuries of Christianity in Africa to examine the concurrent centuries in Europe—we find the Romans of these centuries mainly worshipping the state's traditional gods, Stoicism, or Zoroastrianism.[1] Further, it is

---

[1] Stoicism, Universal Standard Encyclopedia Vol. XVIII, p. 218 & Birley, A., Marcus Aurelius pp. 126 - 134 & Griggs, C., Early Egyptian Christianity: From its Origins to 451 C.E. p. 21 & Hyde, W., Paganism to Christianity in the Roman Empire pp. 28, 59 - 61 & Sykes, E., Everyman's Dictionary of Non-classical Mythology pp. 4 - 5 & Frank, T., A History of Rome pp. 511 - 512 & Higgins, G., Anacalypsis Vol. II, p. 99 & Zoroastrian Religion, Encyclopedia of Religion Vol. XV, p. 556 - 559 & Comte, F., Mythology p. 27, 39 & Budge, E.A., A History of Egypt Vol. VII, pp. 68 - 69

The Stoic Philosophy was created by the Phoenician Zeno and taught to the Athenians during the 4th century BCE. The doctrine was a combination of ethics, physics, and logic. Stoics also saw the expression of human emotions as a hindrance to philosophical realization, and placed little emphasis on the soul and afterlife. Such noted Romans as Seneca, Epictetus, and Marcus Aurelius were adherents of the creed. In the 6th century BCE., the Elamites began to embrace the worship of Zoroastrianism. The religion's founder was the Prophet Zarathushtra (Zoroaster). Zarathushtra's Gathas (a religious text of poetic compositions) was celebrated throughout the Old World. This religion considered Ahura Mazda (Lord of Knowledge) to be a Supreme Being who was embroiled in an epic struggle against Anra Mainyut (King of Evil). Ahura Mazda and Anra Mainyut were said to be the twin sons of Zervan Akarana. Interestingly, he was depicted as an eagle with outstretched wings (similar to Egypt's Ra). Other deities of the faith were the Mother Goddess Pinikir and the Sun-God Mithra. Mithra was said to have been born

Constantine & Christianity

clear that the Europeans who inhabited the continent's more northern and westerly reaches were still practicing their Norse, Druid, or Earth (Mother) and Sky (Father) religions. Even more, scholars explain that those Europeans who were not under the yoke of these beliefs—had no well established organized religion, *to speak of*, at all. The fact is that these were not ancient regions of great spiritual tradition, temples, or shrines.

Consequently, <u>the principle vehicle for the spread of Christianity in Europe was not an affinity for a new spiritual doctrine, or even missionary zeal</u>—**but fire and the sword**![2] Over and above that, *in relative terms,* the continent's bloody conversion began quite late. For instance, Charlemagne would not begin forcibly converting the Saxons to Christianity until the end of the 8th century CE. These observations about Charlemagne's murderous campaign by Robinson, epitomize the spread of the religion in Northern Europe:

---

on December 25th, put to death, and resurrected on the 25th of March. He was also one of the deities that judged men's souls: some souls went to heaven; some went to hell; and others went to a region that was in between. Because the Elamites possessed one of the world's most adept cultures and powerful armies of the period—many of their customs came to have a profound effect upon the Romans. For instance, it is not uncommon to find many Romans commemorating Mithra as a young man killing a bull, which symbolized the god's victory over death.
[2] Davis, E., <u>The First Sex</u> pp. 238 - 239

Africa's Indispensable Role

> *"They knew that the profession of Christianity would be followed by the building of churches and that the churches which the missionaries would build would in course of time become centres of villages and eventually of towns subject to a stable form of government. Unwilling as they were to abandon their roving and migratory habits, it was but natural that they [the Saxons] should vehemently oppose the spread of Christianity in their midst . . ."*

He continues:

> *"It is true that the Saxons respected neither sex nor age and massacred nearly all the inhabitants of the districts which they overran, but the Christian king was no whit behind them in ruthlessness and perfidy, and on one occasion he massacred in cold blood, at Verden on the R. Aller, four thousand Saxon warriors who had surrendered . . . When, however, a campaign was over and the carnage was completed, he would send for clergy to baptize the survivors and to enroll them as members of the Christian church."*[3]

---

[3] Robinson, C., The Conversion of Europe pp. 380 - 381, 386 - 387 & Simons, G., Barbarian Europe pp. 102 - 103

The Saxons consisted of three large migratory tribes known as the Ostphalians, Westphalians, and Angarians. They occupied much of the region now considered Northern Germany.

Constantine & Christianity

<u>Contrasting these findings with Christianity's peaceful proliferation throughout Ethiopia 400 years earlier—leaves one at a total loss for words.</u>

Nevertheless, the first state in Europe to officially accept the Christian Religion was the Roman Empire in the 4th century CE. Becoming Emperor of the Western Empire in 306 CE., Flavius Valerius Aurelius Constantinus (Constantine I) is commonly considered to be Europe's first Christian ruler. Though born and reared in the pagan traditions of Roman society, Constantine is said to have had a vision of a great cross in the sky before going into battle against his fellow countryman Maxentius, on the Milivian Bridge in 312 CE. It is to be noted that the veracity of this tale has often been called into question, because the narrative of Constantine's vision was first advanced by Christian writers who wrote about the episode many years after the battle. That aside, in light of Constantine's resounding victory and the death of Maxentius, his triumph is considered to be a pivotal moment in the establishment of the Christian Religion in Rome.[4]

---

[4] <u>Universal Standard Encyclopedia</u> Vol. V, pp. 1793 - 1794, Vol. VI, p. 1962 & Constantine, <u>Encyclopedia of Religion</u> Vol. IV, p. 70 & Greece, <u>Collier's Encyclopedia</u> Vol. XI, p. 407 & Robinson, C., <u>The Conversion of Europe</u> pp. 188 - 189 & Clovis I, <u>Encyclopedia of Early Christianity</u> p. 219
The date of Constantine's conversion to Christianity is also considered as Greece's, even though the traditional gods of the Greeks were actually worshipped on the peninsula well into the 7th century CE. That being said, in all honesty we

Africa's Indispensable Role

What perverse irony: **the same state that murdered blameless Christians for centuries would now begin to place crosses on their weaponry and spend the ensuing centuries spilling the blood of non-believers in the so-called name of Christianity.** When one reflects upon the earlier Christian instruction of such great African figures as Clement of Alexandria, one cannot help but to be struck by this perversion of the true doctrine. For instance, as Dean of Egypt's Catechetical Institute, Clement taught the following: *"With the attainment of Christian perfection, the individual, is neither restrained by fear that God*

---

find martial considerations playing a role in the religious conversion of several of Europe's leaders. For example, military considerations would play a part in the Khazarian King Bulan's decision to convert his people to Judaism. Further, Gregory of Tours explained that at a critical point in a difficult battle against the Alemanni—the pagan Clovis of the Franks stopped to petition the God of the Christians. He declared that if the God would grant the Franks victory he would convert the Franks to Christianity. The bishop continues that shortly after the prayer—the Alemanni turned and fled. Amazed by this, Clovis had himself and some 3,000 troops baptized as Christians in 496 CE. Clovis I is considered the paramount figure in the spread of Christianity over the western half of the European Continent. The truth is Christianity's spread across Western Europe was far from immediate—**being both slow and violent.** What's more, even in the territories where churches were established, most Western Europeans had no understanding of the Latin tongue. Thus, the Latin scriptures were just as foreign to Northwestern Europeans as the earlier Hebrew, Aramaic, and Egyptian scriptures had been to the Romans (see page 55).

will punish the wicked nor motivated by the hope that he will reward the obedient, for devotion has become a free and spontaneous expression of life wholly consecrated to the Divine reality."[5]

These are sentiments that were, doubtlessly, never truly processed by Constantine. Moreover, it goes without saying that the first Christians did not view their lives as a chance to amass material wealth—or impose their will upon others through martial force and/or threat of murder. Their purpose was to humbly endure, and if necessary suffer, the trials and temptations of this life so that they might be edified, and receive the ultimate reward of life everlasting!

That all said, even after obtaining his military victory—Constantine's acceptance of the Faith's tenets was hardly immediate; and the same would also be so of his empire. Indeed, while Constantine enacted the Edict of Milan in 313 C.E., (*a decree making it possible for a Roman citizen to legally worship any religion they chose without fear of*

---

[5] Burkill, T., The Evolution of Christian Thought p. 66 & Seldes, G., The Great Quotations p. 193

Incidentally, Clement would also exhort the Coptic Christian community to guard against greed and materialism: *"The use of all things that are found in this world ought to be common to all men. Only the most manifest iniquity makes one say to the other, 'This belongs to me, that to you.' Hence the origin of contention among men."*

Africa's Indispensable Role

state persecution) he personally kept the title of <u>Pontifex Maximus</u>: a term of ancient Babylonian origin, in effect, designating himself the High Priest of all of the traditional gods of the Roman Empire. No less telling, while the Emperor is not reported to have been a participant in any of Rome's pagan ceremonies after 312 CE., it is clear that these state rituals would continue well into his reign. In actual point of fact, Constantine didn't attempt to curb any of these ancient rites before 324 CE.[6] In deference here to Bowder: *"Under Constantine, Roman society was still pagan in majority, including a very large majority of the governing classes, and the religion of office-holders reflected this . . . even*

---

[6] Constantine, <u>Encyclopedia of Religion</u> Vol. IV, p. 70 & Constantine I, <u>The New Columbia Encyclopedia</u> p. 634 & <u>Marcus Aurelius and His Times</u> p. 115 & Birley, A., <u>Marcus Aurelius</u> p. 331 & Higgins, G., <u>Anacalypsis</u> Vol. II, p. 51

A large part of Constantine's motivation to appease the Christians may have been to bolster Christian support for his eastern campaign against Licinius. Remember, by this time large numbers of Christians existed in the African and Asian provinces. Additionally, long before the reign of Constantine, Roman emperors were to commemorate the resolve of Hebrew and Christian martyrs: *Marcus Aurelius setting Christians apart from many others—describing them as a group that was not afraid to die!* Having pierced the Roman psyche, it was just a matter of time before an emperor would try to harness this spiritual conviction for some corporeal advantage. Lo and behold, a powerful story about the young Constantine receiving a divinely inspired vision of the Christian cross in a dream the night before courageously joining, *and winning*, the very military battle that would make him Emperor of the Roman Empire!

Constantine & Christianity

at the very end of Constantine's reign the vast majority of the provincial governors were pagans."[7]

This is a gold medallion of Constantine with Sol Invictus. The phrase *Sol Invictus* means, "The Invincible Sun." It is noteworthy that this metal was minted by the Romans in 313 CE., which is after Constantine's public conversion to Christianity.

---

[7] Pfeffer, L., Church, State, And Freedom p. 13 & Hyde, W., Paganism to Christianity in the Roman Empire p. 34 & Bowder, D., The Age of Constantine and Julian p. 95
In this instance, the term *pagan* denotes someone who is polytheistic (see page 34).

Africa's Indispensable Role

Despite these irrefutable historical findings, there are still many writers in the West, who erroneously point to Constantine I as the figure who instantly transformed Rome into a shimmering beacon of European Christianity in the 4th century! In light of this blunder, I am compelled to take a moment to touch upon the life, *and actual behavior*, of Constantine the Great—so that you might be able to evaluate his character and commitment to the tenets of the Christian Religion, *or lack thereof*, for yourself:[8]

---

[8] Constantine the Great, Encyclopedia of Early Christianity p. 326 & Constantine I, Universal Standard Encyclopedia Vol. VI, p. 1962 & Davis, E., The First Sex pp. 232 - 238 & Walker, B., The Woman's Encyclopedia of Myths and Secrets p. 820 & Bowder, D., Who was Who in the Roman World p. 106 & Frank, T., A History of Rome p. 562 & Constantine I, The New Columbia Encyclopedia p. 634 & Grant, M., The Roman Emperors pp. 227 - 234 & Boak, A., & Sinnigen, W., A History of Rome to A.D. 565 pp. 502 - 507 & Millar, F., The Emperor in the Roman World pp. 584 - 607 & Pfeffer, L., Church, State, And Freedom p. 14 & Du Bourguet, P., Early Christian Painting p. 10 & Harnack, A., The Mission and Expansion of Christianity in the first three centuries Vol. II, p. 75 & Hastings, J., Selbie, J., & Lambert, J., Dictionary of the Apostolic Church & Guillamont, A., The Gospel According to Thomas p. 19 & Kidd, B., Documents Illustrative of the History of the Church Vol. II p. 7 & Higgins, G., Anacalypsis Vol. I, p. 331, Vol. II, p. 51, 89 - 90 & Hyde, W., Paganism to Christianity in the Roman Empire p. 257 & Exodus 31:12-18 & Ward, P., A Dictionary of Common Fallacies p. 249

Thomas records the Christ as saying: *"If you keep not the Sabbath as Sabbath, you will not see the Father."*

Constantine & Christianity

Through the ages, historians have differed about the early life of Helena, who was the mother of Constantine. While some writers, *incredibly*, portray her as a Christian Princess of a tribe of Britons—others explain that she was a prostitute from Dacia (region of ancient Rumania). However, less speculation exists regarding Constantine's pagan father, Constantius. He was an accomplished soldier who worked his way up through Rome's military ranks. Coming to obtain favor with his Emperor, Constantius was eventually given the hand of Theodora, the stepdaughter of a nobleman. Constantius and Theodora had two sons by the time that Constantius met Helena and sired Constantine. Though considered as illegitimate by many, the young Constantine would be allowed to follow in his father's military footsteps. Upon Constantius' death in 306 CE., we find that Constantine would become Caesar of the West over Theodora's children.

As Emperor, Constantine is believed to have had a hand in the death of his father-in-law Maximian in 310 CE.

To insure his unchallenged reign, in 326 CE., he had his son Crispus murdered.

Even though she is routinely declared to have been innocent of the charge by ancient chroniclers—Constantine, with the aid of his mother Helena, *whom he determined should be made a Saint*, had

Africa's Indispensable Role

his second wife Fausta declared an adulterer and killed. Davis writes:

> "The **Catholic Encyclopedia** *fails to mention the fact that Constantine scalded his young wife to death in a cauldron of water brought to a slow boil over a wood fire—a protracted and agonizing death indeed. Nor does it mention Saint Helena's part in the crime.*"

Not stopping there, he also had a hand in the death of one of his nephews.

While we know Constantine was willing to call great councils in which the Christian leaders would deliberate over the proper course of the Church—it is also clear that he generally moved slow, *if at all*, to enforce these councils' mandates. Consequently, these assemblies didn't carry the momentous significance one might imagine; even within the body of the Church. Point in fact: while admittedly difficult issues, neither the Synod of Arles called in 314 CE. to settle the Donatist controversy—nor the Council of Nicea convened in 325 CE. to address the doctrine of Arius, would be able to establish policies that would be adhered to throughout the Church's hierarchy.

Although I cannot speak to the religious sincerity of his enactment of the policy—Constantine's political determination that the Church hierarchy should be

Constantine & Christianity

treated as an arm of his governmental administration, also did little to enhance the acceptance of Christ's true teachings throughout the empire. In truth, granting the clergy authority over the civil courts, and giving them large monetary purses, did little more than lead to abuse . . .

As the Emperor was also amenable to the idea of male superiority, the environment for heightened doctrinal sexism in the Faith was also able to take hold in the 4th century CE. However, I want to be clear here—such opinions were not universally held by the Church leaders of earlier times. For instance, a passage from Tertullian's de Anima states:
> *"We have with us a sister who has had a share in the spiritual gifts of revelation. For in church, during the Sabbath worship, she undergoes ecstasies. She converses with angels, at times even with the Lord himself; she sees and hears mysteries, pierces the hearts of several people, and suggests remedies to those who desire them."*

Atop this, the Emperor did not merely institute the earlier pagan practice of cremation into Rome's Christian mainstream against the wishes of the Church Fathers—but he went so far as to change the holy day of the Christian Sabbath (Exodus 16:23 – 16:29) from its original Saturday to Sunday! In an edict entitled, Constantine's Legislation about Sunday, 321 A.D., we find this pronouncement:

Africa's Indispensable Role

> *"Constantine to Elpidius.—All judges and city-people and the craftsmen shall rest upon the venerable Day of the Sun. Country-people, however, may freely attend to the cultivation of the fields, because it frequently happens that no other days are better adapted for planting the grain in furrows or the vines in trenches; so that the advantage given by heavenly providence may not, for the occasion of a short time, perish. Given on March 7 [321], in the second consulate of Crispus and the second of Constantine."*

<u>Evidently, YHVH's instruction to Moses, 2,000 years of Hebraic tradition, and almost 300 years of Christian custom—was less important to Constantine than maintaining the Roman religious tradition of observing the Sabbath on the first day of the week: the *Dies Solis* ("Day of the Sun").</u>

Finally here, the respected Sir Godfrey Higgins describes Rome's conversion to Christianity thusly:

> *"It must be recollected that we are in the very centre of the era of frauds, of every kind, and that he, that is, his church, was able to destroy, and did destroy, everything which it did not approve. It could corrupt what it pleased, and we scarcely possess a single writing which it ordered to be destroyed, which is a sufficient proof of its power to affect its wicked designs. Constantine was, in fact, both Pagan and Christian; and his*

97

Constantine & Christianity

> *church, as I will prove, was more an union of the two, than a substitution of one for the other."*

After one stops to reflect upon the difficult sacrifices made by so many Africans for the early Faith—it becomes clear that the conversion to the religion by Constantine and the Romans was neither as perilous, nor admirable. In closing, allow me to leave you with this remark by Pfeffer about Constantine the man:

> *"Although not baptized—at least not until he was on his deathbed—Constantine was undoubtedly personally sympathetic to Christianity. But his actions were primarily motivated not by that sympathy, but by political considerations. Again religion became an engine of state policy. For Constantine considered Christianity as a means of unifying his complex empire. As Pontifex Maximus of the non-Christian state religion, he of course had exclusive power to control its administration and its course. Constantine and his successors had no hesitation in exercising the same control of the newly recognized religion and according it the same favors previously enjoyed by its predecessor."*[9]

---

[9] Pfeffer, L., <u>Church, State, And Freedom</u> p. 14

Africa's Indispensable Role

Fourth century bust of Constantine I

Constantine & Christianity

Theodosius & the Official Mandate of 383 CE.

It is manifest that the Roman populace did not turn to the Christian Religion during the 4th century with the same vigor as 1st, 2nd, and 3rd century Africans! If the truth is to be told, the empire would continue its pagan worship for decades after Constantine's edict. But in 383 CE., the Emperor Theodosius decided that Catholicism should become the preeminent religion of the state. Historians explain that although genuinely moved by the Faith, a large part of Theodosius' motivation for a societal conversion may well have been his desire to alleviate the burden of costly pagan ceremonies and sacrifices upon the Roman treasury.

In any event, Theodosius determined that Catholic bishops, *whose appointments should be made by him*, would control all of the empire's churches. While the Church hierarchy accepted the idea of controlling the churches, they would reject the emperor's offer of controlling their appointments. However, during Theodosius' reign, bishops would become an even greater part of the state apparatus than under Constantine. Before long, the Church became an arm of the state—with Bishop Nestor persuading Theodosius to enact the following religious decrees: <u>Christian heretics could not build</u>

Africa's Indispensable Role

<u>churches, hold assemblies, or teach their doctrines (even privately); pagans were required to be baptized and attend church services; and those persons who would not adhere to these conditions were to be exiled, or put to death</u>! The general ambiance of the empire's Christianity is probably best expressed here:

> *"When Nestor was consecrated Bishop of Constantinople, he preached a sermon to the Emperor Theodosius in which he said: 'Give me, my Prince, the earth purged of heretics, and I will give you heaven as a recompense. Assist me in destroying heretics, and I will assist you in vanquishing the Persians.'"*[10]

Yet and still, even with the official 4th century decree of Theodosius that Christianity was the only religion that could be worshipped in the empire, in truth, large segments of the state's populace still remained pagan. In the words of Robinson:

> *"The last stronghold of heathenism in Rome was the Roman Senate. Its members represented the traditions and the glories of the past. Moreover, the city was full of temples, many of which had been built to*

---

[10] Robinson, C., <u>The Conversion of Europe</u> p. 219 & MacMullen, R., <u>Christianizing the Roman Empire A.D. 100 - 400</u> pp. 55 - 56 & Grant, M., <u>The Roman Emperors</u> p. 272 & Du Bourguet, P., <u>Early Christian Painting</u> p. 44 & Crucitti, E., <u>Rome Pagan and Christian: The Persecutions</u> & Pfeffer, L., <u>Church, State, And Freedom</u> p. 14

Constantine & Christianity

commemorate victories, and the senate was specially concerned to preserve intact the religious ceremonies connected with them. Paganism in fact remained the state religion of Rome till 383, and well on into the fifth century it was represented in Rome by some of its leading citizens . . ."[11]

View of the celebrated Roman Forum from the Arch of Lucius Septimius Severus.

---

[11] Robinson, C., The Conversion of Europe p. 219

The Blossoming of Christianity in Ethiopia

Blossoming in Ethiopia

This fresco portrays the Queen of Sheba being protected on her journey from Ethiopia to Jerusalem, to be received by King Solomon of the Hebrews in the 10th century BCE. Both—a historical chronicle of the Queen's experience with King Solomon, and the final locale of the Ark of the Covenant—are discussed in Ethiopia's Kebra Negast!

Africa's Indispensable Role

Allow me to say a word about the famed Ethiopians. It has already been established that from the 1st through the 4th centuries CE.—Ethiopia's commitment to Christianity would far exceed that of the Romans. Additionally here, ancient chroniclers explain that the material and cultural standards of this African kingdom were on par with the Romans. Truth be told, while the Romans were able to cause great havoc in Egypt and Northern Africa, they did not even attempt to invade the lands of the celebrated Ethiopians!

However, as the Pharaonic era was to run its three-millennium course in Ethiopia, we come to the emergence of three separate formal Christian kingdoms. Chroniclers explain that an African people called the Nobatae, who were from the Ethiopian desert, migrated east to settle along the banks of the Nile. From their new home, they would eventually overcome the Blemmye (the area's older inhabitants).[1] Once checking the Blemmye, these new settlers would establish the state of Nobatia.

---

[1] De Graft-Johnson, J., African Glory p. 48 & Keating, R., Nubian Twilight p. 75 & Shinnie, P., Meroe p. 56

It is also to be noted that Rome's Diocletian supported the Nobataean move into the region. This was because the Nobataeans slowed the raiding of the Blemmyeans against Roman troops in Southern Egypt. As the Blemmye worshipped Isis and other traditional Nile Valley gods, they took offense and often attacked Roman troops stationed near the Southern temples of such gods as Isis, Osiris, and Horus.

Blossoming in Ethiopia

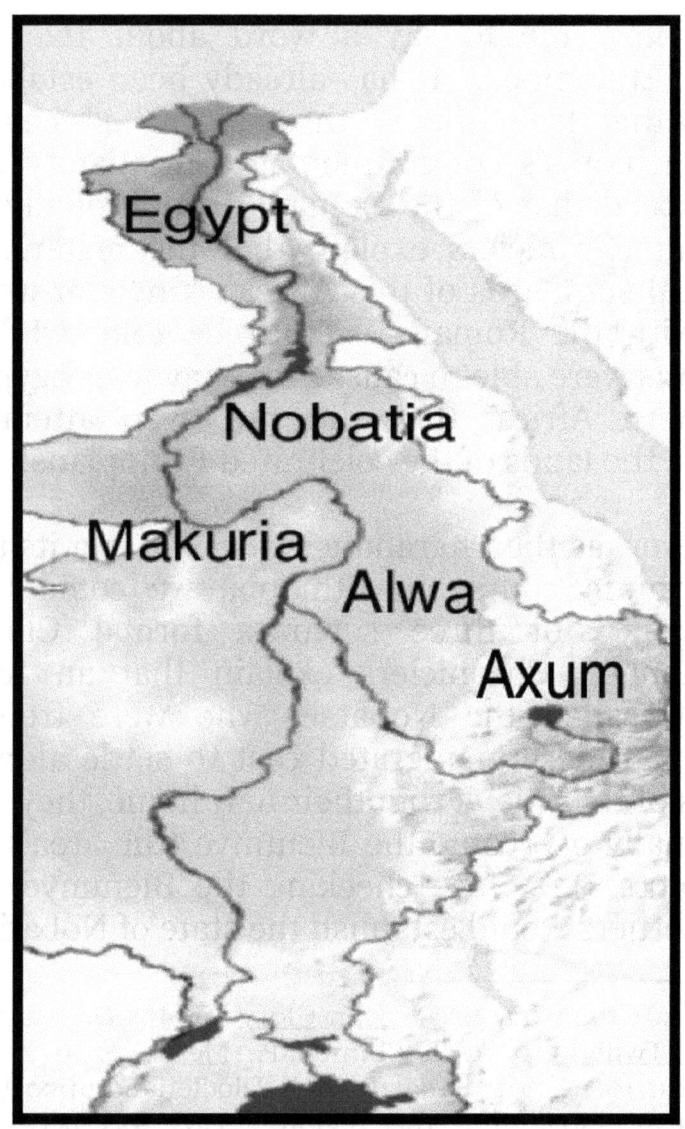

The Nile River Valley is over 4,000 miles long. Here are the Christian kingdoms that had evolved, **_and were flourishing_**, along the banks of the Nile by the 7th century CE.

Africa's Indispensable Role

In brief, the emergence of the Nobatae, coupled with a lessening from the more authoritative policies of the ancient Pharaonic kings of the South—led to a period that would give rise to three more regional powers along the banks of the Southern Valley. Thus, by the 6th century CE., the Southern Nile was home to three fairly distinct new states: Nobatia (stretching from the 1st to the 3rd cataracts of the Nile); Makuria (located between the 4th and 5th cataracts); and Alwa (which occupied the area of the Blue Nile southeast of Khartoum).

But even with these territorial changes, Axum's overall martial prowess is still evidenced through the fact that during the 6th century CE., the Roman Emperor Justinian would openly seek a military alliance with these Africans of the Southern Nile. What's more, further proof of Ethiopia's strength is to be garnered from King Kaleb's crushing defeat of Dhu Nuwas on the Sinai Peninsula: the affect of which, was Axum's continued sway over much of the Southwestern Sinai. However, *both remarkable and revealing*, Ethiopian tradition explains that King Kaleb would ultimately abdicate the throne for his Faith! *It is said that after first giving his crown to the Church of the Holy Sepulchre in Jerusalem—he would then retire to a Christian monastery where he would embrace the lifestyle of a monk.*[2]

---

[2] Metzger, B., The Early Version of the New Testament pp. 268 - 269 & Hansberry, L., Pillars in Ethiopian History pp. 100 - 107 & Taylor, J., Egypt and Nubia pp. 60 - 64 &

Blossoming in Ethiopia

The Church of the Holy Sepulchre in Jerusalem

Doresse, J., Ethiopia pp. 86 – 88 & Munro-Hay, S., Aksum: An African Civilization of Late Antiquity
According to the ancient Palestinian historian Procopius, King Kaleb's Ethiopian name was Ella Asbeha, which means "The One who Brought the Morning." By the beginning of the 8th century CE., Nobatia and Makuria would merge to form one great territorial State. The Church of the Holy Sepulchre is venerated as the *Golgotha* ("Place where the Messiah was Buried").

Africa's Indispensable Role

Yet, despite the emergence of these new states in Eastern Africa—what's found is that the worship of the Christian Religion did not wane throughout the Southern Nile! For example:[3]

Many of early Christianity's most celebrated Saints were Ethiopians of this age—Zamik-el, Pantalewon, Afse, Yeshaq, and the heralded Yared of the 6th century—all immediately come to mind!

Indeed, after his travels throughout the Southern Nile, the Greek Monk Cosmas Indicopleustes would testify that there were churches, *"everywhere!"*

Further, the celebrated Saint Jerome was to proclaim that the monks of Ethiopia were Standard-Bearers of the Faith: actually referring to them as, **"lilies of purity!"**

---

[3] De Graft-Johnson, J., African Glory p. 48 & Keating, R., Nubian Twilight p. 76 & Metzger, B., The Early Version of the New Testament p. 221 & Ethiopian Church, Encyclopedia of Religion Vol. V, p. 174 & Budge, E.A., The Book of the Saints of the Ethiopian Church & Hansberry, L., Pillars in Ethiopian History pp. 87 - 88, 95, 97 - 99 & Doresse, J., Ethiopia pp. 85 - 96, 117 - 120, 205 & The Coptic Encyclopedia & Cox, G., African Empires and Civilizations p. 119, 121 & Taylor, J., Egypt and Nubia p. 64 & Greenfield, R., Ethiopia
The granite dimensions of Medhave Alem are 112 by 80 feet. Lalibela was also the site of several other wonderful churches and Debra Damo: one of the Old World's most heralded regions of monastic Christianity (see pages 49 and 50).

Blossoming in Ethiopia

We even have John Taylor commemorating the history of the Faith in Ethiopia thusly: *"The eight to nine centuries of the Christian era was a period of growth and prosperity in both political and cultural spheres . . ."*

Now contrast the preceding remarks with this statement by Gerald Simons, about the spread of the Christian Religion in Western Europe during the concurrent centuries:

"It took the [Catholic] Church centuries . . . to teach the true meaning of the Faith and bring the religious practices of its congregants into accord with Christian belief. The problem of religious indoctrination had been a frustrating one for the Church since the first Germanic barbarians were baptized. While those superstitious warriors eagerly embraced Christianity as a superior cult, many of them also clung to their traditional pagan war-gods and nature-spirits. Zealous churchmen found that it did little good to destroy pagan shrines. The new Faith and the old one tended to coexist, and were practiced alternately or simultaneously . . ."[4]

---

[4] Owen, F., The Germanic People p. 109 & Simons, G., Barbarian Europe p. 88 & Von Ranke, L., A History of England Vol. I, pp. 12 - 13 & Druids, The American Peoples Encyclopedia Vol. VII, p. 342 & France, The World Book Encyclopedia Vol. VII, p. 471 & Rogers, J.A., Sex and Race Vol. III, p. 4

Africa's Indispensable Role

In winding up, it would be an oversight not to say a word about Lalibela of the Ethiopian highlands. In ancient times, this city would serve as a hub for many of the Faith's most heralded African followers. Considered the Jerusalem of Ethiopia, Lalibela (also known as Roha) was widely held as the region where Adam (the first man) lived and was buried. That aside, many of this center's spiritual leaders trace their ancestry back to Moses and Solomon! The largest church of this region of stone churches was called *Medhave Alem*, which means "Savior of the World." Jean Doresse would write the following about the culture and spirituality of the Ethiopians:

> *"Religion is at the core of Ethiopian civilization, which stems from Old Testament tradition no less than from the teachings of Christ. Again and again the Ethiopians have seemed to turn aside from the temptations of worldly wealth or to devote their riches outright to the glory of God. For this reason, with few exceptions, they have left behind them churches and convents rather than palaces."*

Ironically, Europe's Teutonic conversion to Roman Catholicism would loosely mirror the Roman adoption of the Faith from the earlier African Church (e.g., see page 55). Perhaps, nothing illustrates this observation better than the fact that the Roman Church of the Middle Ages felt compelled to summarily ban marriages between Rome's Catholic citizens and the Scandinavians, Germans, and Britons because of these Teutons unwillingness to discontinue their heathenism.

Blossoming in Ethiopia

This is a fresco of the Black Madonna and Christ child. This icon is housed today in an Axum Church.

Africa's Indispensable Role

The Later Martyrs of Ethiopia

Unfortunately, the Egyptians, Numidians, and Carthaginians were not the only Africans who would be forced to make the ultimate sacrifice for the Faith—insomuch as the state-sanctioned murder of Christians would be a habit that the Romans would find hard to break. **_Incredibly, in the 17th century, Roman Catholics persecuted and murdered tens of thousands of heroic Ethiopian Christians!_** The dastardly crime of these Ethiopian Christians was that they would not disavow their ancient Christian traditions for the customs of the Roman Catholic Church.

Briefly, by the 15th century, Ethiopian rulers had begun to look to Portugal for assistance against the expansion minded forces of Islam in Africa. The Portuguese were amenable to the idea of supporting the Ethiopians because it would also create an opportunity to bring them under the yoke of Catholicism and the Pope. However, the corporeal designs of the Portuguese would hit a spiritual snag in Ethiopia. As Frumentius (Ethiopia's first Abun) was ordained by the Bishop of Alexandria during the 4th century CE.—the Ethiopians considered themselves a part of the Coptic (or Jacobite) Church of Egypt. Hence, the Ethiopians did not consider

Blossoming in Ethiopia

the Papacy of Rome to have any spiritual standing, when it came to their doctrinal affairs.

Portuguese martial assistance or not—the Ethiopian populace remained unwilling to consider embracing the peculiar spiritual tenets of the Roman Catholic Pope. A religious chasm soon developed which came to a head in the 17th century. During the episcopacy of the Catholic Jesuit Afonso Mendez (c.1625) several controversial policies were enacted and enforced: (1) Ethiopians were commanded to swear their undivided allegiance to the Roman Pope; (2) it was mandated that the traditional day of the Sabbath (Saturday) would be changed to that of the Romans (Sunday); (3) male circumcision was suspended; (4) church altars were ordered redesigned and their priests had to either be removed or re-ordained; (5) the dates of several feast days were changed; and (6), members of the Ethiopian congregation had to repeat the rite of Christian baptism.

Needless to say, the Roman Church's demands meant little to the Ethiopians in the face of over 1300 years of Christian tradition. Unbelievably, once again, the deplorable Roman response would be to murder those Africans who would not acquiesce. After the deaths of thousands of Ethiopian Christians, the Catholic edicts were rescinded, as it was clear that the masses would rather die than adopt the alien practices of the

Africa's Indispensable Role

foreign, *and unorthodox*, Church.⁵ In a tribute to the timeless devotion and laudable character of the African Christians of Ethiopia, Bruce declares:

"No war to introduce it, no fanatical Priesthood to oppose it, no bloodshed to disgrace it; Its only argument was its truth . . . its only ornament was its simplicity . . . men flocked in peaceful humility, and hand and hand, joined cheerfully in doctrines which gave glory to God in the Highest, and announced on earth peace, [and] goodwill toward men."⁶

---

⁵ Marcus, H., A History of Ethiopia pp. 39 - 40 & Budge, E.A., A History of Ethiopia pp. 390 - 394 & Hansberry, L., Pillars in Ethiopian History p. 145 & Ethiopian Catholics, The New Catholic Encyclopedia Vol. V, p. 588 & Ethiopian Church, Encyclopedia of Religion Vol. V, pp. 173 - 175 & Cox, G., African Empires and Civilizations p. 123 & Ethiopian Heresies and Theological Controversies, The Coptic Encyclopedia Vol. III, p. 986 & Doresse, J., Ethiopia pp. 156 – 159

⁶ Hansberry, L., Pillars in Ethiopian History p. 74, 112 & Davis, E., The First Sex p. 239 & Von Ranke, L., History of England Vol. I & Chadwick, N., The Beginnings of Russian History & Carsten, F., The Origins of Prussia & Dictionary of the Middle Ages Vol. X & Crusades, The American Peoples Encyclopedia Vol. VI, pp. 559 - 562

Bruce's observation is underscored here by Robertson: *"The Europeans were never persuaded, never convinced, never won by the appeal of the new doctrine; they were either transformed by their kings to the Church like so many cattle, or beaten down into submission after generations of resistance and massacre. The misery and butchery wrought from first to last are unimaginable . . ."* And God forbid, I

Blossoming in Ethiopia

In conclusion, there can be no doubt that a tremendous debt is owed to the Africans who selflessly carried the blood-stained banner of the early Faith! Despite the fact that many of you have been told that the African was totally ignorant about Christianity until some version of it was imposed upon them by White slaveholders and/or missionaries—nothing could be further from the truth. **Quite frankly, the argument is to be made that at the core of the survival of the Christian Religion is the devotion and sacrifice of millions of courageous Africans!**

Naturally, I make no apology for proclaiming these facts forasmuch as the scriptures teach: *"God is a Spirit; and they that worship Him must worship Him in spirit and in truth!"* So, as we conclude this look at Africa's role in the establishment of the Faith, let me leave you with these words by Wellard:

> "Christianity eventually triumphed over paganism at the beginning of the fourth century, to become the official religion of the Roman Empire. It was nowhere as flourishing as in Africa, where over 2,000 Christian communities have been identified and the names of 1,500 bishops, priests,

---

should chronicle the blood shed in Europe during the introduction of Christianity into England, Scandinavia, Prussia (Northern Germany), and Pomerania (Poland); the Crusades (a series of seven European wars to take Jerusalem and convert the Moslems to Christianity); or, the Inquisition.

Africa's Indispensable Role

deacons, and others have been traced in documents and epitaphs. But these figures are undoubtedly incomplete, since a thorough archaeological survey has never been made, and all that the French historians could do during their occupation of the North African territories was to identify the more obvious churches, chapels, monasteries, cemeteries, tombs, and inscriptions which have survived above ground. How much evidence remains hidden, it is impossible to say."[7]

This is a photo of eight 19th century Coptic Priests. As you can see, the ancient African connection with the first Followers of the Way was never broken . . .

---

[7] John 4: 24 & Wellard, J., Lost Worlds of Africa p. 120

Epilogue:

First, I hope that you have enjoyed reading Africa's Indispensable Role as much as I have delighted in bringing it to you! But to wind this effort up—you will recall that we were forced to begin our journey with the deplorable elephant in the room: **Racism** (see page vii). However, now that the stark contrast between historical fact and modern perception has been made manifest—*Africa, I pray that the truth of the ages will once more stir, and embolden, your spiritual hearts and minds—because loving hearts, and keen minds, can achieve anything that's sanctioned by the* **Lord** *of* **Lords** *and* **King** *of* **Kings***!*

Africa's Indispensable Role

The Souls of the Martyrs is a painting that was created by Spain's Pedro during the 11th century CE. It would be represented in the **Martyrologium Romanum** (a manuscript that was commissioned by the Roman Catholic Church in the 16th century to serve as an official registry of the *early* and *later* canonized Saints and Martyrs of the Faith). Juxtaposed with the Christian art produced by Westerners in these times—it is noteworthy that this Spanish Master of the Middle Ages depicts a greater number of Black, as opposed to White, Catholic Saints and Martyrs.

Epilogue

According to the heralded North African theologian Saint Augustine: "To conquer truly, is to overcome all of the contrivances of your enemy . . ."

Africa's Indispensable Role

Here is an ancient Italian fresco of Saint Augustine. Dating to the 6th century CE., this work of art is housed in Lateran Rome. It is said to be the earliest illustration of the brilliant African Church Father!

Language Word Chart

English	Akkadian	Aramaic	Hebrew	Ethiopic
Water	Mu	Mayya	Mayya	May
Sky	Samu	S-Mayya	Samu-yim	Samay
House	B-tu	Bayta	Bayl	Bet
Name	Sumu	S-ma	Sem	Sem
Head	Resu	Resa	Ro's	Re'es
Peace	Salamu	S-lama	Salom	Salam

Here is a small, but clear, example of the obvious similarity that exists between common words of the ancient Akkadian, Aramaic, Hebrew, and Ethiopian languages. Of course, the English language is not a part of this ancient Black language family.

* To whomever it may concern: The actual ancient Hebrew name of the "Anointed One" was written, YHSVH. This name means, "YHVH Saves" or "YHVH is Salvation" (YHVH being Yahweh in ancient Hebrew). Now, the scriptures also explain that the name of the "Anointed One," was what made it possible for the apostles to achieve their miracles. THUS, WHEN THE APOSTLES WERE PERFORMING SAID—"YOD-HEY-SHIN-VAV-HEY" WAS THE POWERFUL DECLARATIVE SOUND WAVE OF UNIVERSAL AUTHORITY THEY WERE PROCLAIMING!

As for why this understanding is lost on most today, in brief—all of the letters of the Hebrew alphabet do not have Greek equivalents (see page 14). So, once departing from the original Afro-Asiatic Hebraic tongue, the tonal syllabic, and vibratory expression of YHSVH was altered drastically. What's more, he who was first called, Yod-Hey-Shin-Vav-Hey, would come to be known as *Iesous*, which is pronounced, ee-aa-sous or yea-sous, in Greek. No less consequential, *Iesous* would become the root word for the even later Latin name *Jesus*, which is pronounced gee-zus, in the English language today; hence, all of the confusion.

- Worthy, R.L. YHSVH pp. 46 – 67, 74 - 83

Photo Credits:

Unless otherwise stated, all images in this book are presented courtesy of **The Hall of Records** *- KornerStone Books* ©

Page vii – Elephant in the Room   Original Clipart *courtesy* Ron Leishman

Page viii – Public Domain Artwork by Providence Lithograph Company: Moses Pleads with Israel 1907 WC

Page xi – Public Domain Artifact - Menologion Basileiou: St. Gregory the Wonderworker 11th century CE. WC

Page xii – Diocletian Bust *appears courtesy* G. Dall'Orto WC

Page 13 – English: Coptic Alphabet *appears courtesy* Afanous GFDL

Page 25 – Public Domain Artifact: Papyrus Rylands 458 2nd century BCE. WC

Page 29 – Public Domain Artifact: Chester Beatty Papyri 45 3rd century WC

Page 30 – Public Domain Artifact: Chester Beatty Papyri 46 3rd century WC

Page 33 – Nimrud Ivory - Lion eating man *appears courtesy* Prioyman GFDL

Page 34 – Roman flamen *appears courtesy* Jastrow 3rd century GFDL

Page 41 – Public Domain Artwork: Mark Evangelist 18th century WC

Page 45 – Public Domain Artwork: St. Frumentius Middle Ages WC

Page 46 – King Ezana's Obelisk at Axum *appears courtesy* Pzbinden7 GFDL

Page 49 – Monastery Debra Damo Ethiopia *appears courtesy* Giustino CC-by-2.0

Page 50 – Bet Giyorgis church *appears courtesy* Giustino cc-by-sa-2.0

Page 61 – Public Domain Artwork: Cyprian of Carthage Russian Icon WC

Page 68 – St. Antony's Monastery *appears courtesy* Tentolia WC

Photo Credits:

Page 72 – Public Domain Artwork Russian Fresco in Saviour Cathedral of Chernihiv: Saint Thecla 11ᵗʰ century WC

Page 74 – Papal Insignia *appears courtesy* Gigillio83 WC

Page 78 – Public Domain Artwork Varna Archeological Museum: St. Athanasius of Alexandria c.1600s WC

Page 81 – Public Domain Artwork Fitzwilliam Museum: Augustine of Carthage Simone Martini 14ᵗʰ century WC

Page 92 – Unconquered Constantine *appears courtesy* Jastrow WC

Page 99 – Constantine I *appears courtesy* A. Majanlahti CC-2.0 WC

Page 104 – Public Domain Artwork Nat. Museum Addis Ababa: Queen Sheba WC I

Page 106 – Holy Sepulchre in Jerusalem *appears courtesy* B. Werner GFDL

Page 108 – Watershed of the Nile River *appears courtesy* Imagico CC A-S.A. 2.5

Page 111 – Black Madonna and Christ in Cathedral *appears courtesy* M. Stavrev GFDL

Page 116 – Coptic Priests *appears courtesy* Amer. Colony (Jerusalem) Photo Dept. 1914 WC

Page 118 – Man kicking Elephant to the Curb Original Clipart *courtesy* Ron Leishman

Page 119 – Public Domain Artwork: The Souls of the Martyrs c.1091 CE. Master Pedro WC

Page 120 – Public Domain Artwork Lateran Rome: Augustine c.500 CE. WC

Page 126 – Gero Cross *appears courtesy* elya CC A-S.A. 2.5 GFDL
This crucifix is known as the Gero Cross. It was commissioned in the 10ᵗʰ century, by the Archbishop of Cologne Germany, Gero. Carved out of oak, it stands over six feet tall. This crucifix was the largest sculpture north of the Western European Alps for generations.

Page 138 – Public Domain Artwork Palekh Russia: John the Baptist c.1800s WC

Page 149 – Public Domain Artwork: Mark the Evangelist Emmanuel Tzanes 17ᵗʰ century WC

Page 152 – Public Domain Artwork State Russian Museum: St. George and the Dragon 15ᵗʰ century Novogrod School WC

For the weapons of our warfare are not flesh, but powerful through God, to the pulling down of strongholds; and the casting out of false imaginations . . .

Saint Paul

Africa's Indispensable Role

Bibliography:

Ackroyd, P., & Evans, C., The Cambridge History of the Bible Cambridge Univ. Press 1970

al-Makarim, A., Tarikh al-Kana'is wa-al-Adyirah Cairo 1984

Angus, S., The Environment of Early Christianity Duckworth Co. 1914

Aziz, A., The Coptic Encyclopedia Macmillan Publ. 1991

Birley, A., Marcus Aurelius Little, Brown & Co. 1966

Birley, A., Septimius Severus: The African Emperor Doubleday 1972

Boak, A., & Sinnigen, W., A History of Rome to A.D. 565 Macmillan 1965

Bowder, D., The Age of Constantine and Julian Harper & Row 1978

Bowder, D., Who was Who in the Roman World Cornell Univ. Press 1975

Bibliography

Budge, E.A., A History of Egypt Anthropological Pub. 1968

Budge, E.A., A History of Ethiopia Anthropological Pub. 1966

Budge, E.A., The Book of the Dead Arkana 1985

Budge, E.A., The Book of the Saints of the Ethiopian Church Cambridge Univ. 1928

Budge, E.A., The Dwellers on the Nile Dover 1977

Budge, E.A., The Nile Thos. Cook & Sons 1907

Burghardt, W., Lawler, T., & Dillion, J., Ancient Christian Writers: The Works of the Fathers in Translation Newman 1946

Burkill, T., The Evolution of Christian Thought Cornell Univ. 1971

Burn, A., & Selincourt, A., Herodotus: The Histories Penguin 1954

Carsten, F., The Origins of Prussia Oxford Press 1954

Case, S., Evolution of Early Christianity Univ. of Chicago 1917

Africa's Indispensable Role

Chadwick, N., The Beginnings of Russian History Cambridge Press 1946

Clegg, R., Mackey's Revised History of Freemasonry The Masonic History Co. 1898

Comte, F., Mythology Chambers 1994

Cox, G., African Empires and Civilizations African Heritage Studies Publ. 1974

Crombie, F., The Writings of Origen T & T Clark 1911

Crucitti, E., Rome Pagan and Christian: The Persecutions Crucitti & Raber 1979

Davies, J., Daily Life of Early Christians Duell, Sloan & Pearce 1952

Davis, E., The First Sex Putnam & Sons 1971

De Ferrari, J., The Fathers of the Church: Eusebius Pamphili-Ecclesiastical History Fathers of the Church Inc. 1953

De Graft-Johnson, J., African Glory Black Classic Press 1954

Diggs, E., Black Chronology Hall 1983

Bibliography

Du Bourguet, P., Early Christian Art Reynal 1971

Du Bourguet, P., Early Christian Painting Viking 1965

Ennabli, A., & Slim, H., Carthage: A Visit to the Ruins Ceres Publ. 1987

Farmer, D., The Oxford Dictionary of Saints Clarendon Press 1978, 1982

Ferguson, E., Encyclopedia of Early Christianity Garland 1990

Frank, H., Swain, C., & Canby, C., The Bible Through the Ages World Publ. Co. 1967

Frank, T., A History of Rome Holt 1923

Fremantle, A., A Treasury of Early Christianity Viking 1953

Goodspeed, E., The Story of the New Testament U. of Chic. Press 1916

Grant, M., The Roman Emperors Scribner & Sons 1985

Greenfield, R., Ethiopia Praeger 1968

Africa's Indispensable Role

Griggs, C., Early Egyptian Christianity: From its Origins to 451 C.E. Brill 1991

Groves, C., The Planting of Christianity in Africa Lutterworth Press 1948

Guillamont, A., The Gospel According to Thomas Harper & Bros. 1959, 1984

Hall, M., The Secret Teachings of All Ages The Philosophical Research Soc. 1977

Hamilton, E., Mythology: Timeless Tales of Gods and Heroes New American Library 1940

Hansberry, W., Pillars in Ethiopian History Howard Univ. Press 1974

Harnack, A., The Mission and Expansion of Christianity in the first three centuries Vol. II Williams & Norgate 1908

Hastings, J., Selbie, J., & Lambert, J., Dictionary of the Apostolic Church Scribner 1916

Hefele, C., & Oxenham, H., Canons of the Council of Carthage May 1 418 Patristics in English 2012

Higgins, G., Anacalypsis University Books 1965

Bibliography

Hodgson, M., The Venture of Islam: Conscience and History in a World Civilization U. of Chicago 1974

Hyde, W., Paganism to Christianity in the Roman Empire Univ. of Penn. 1946

Jongeling, K., & Kerr, R., Late Punic Epigraphy Mohr Siebeck 2005

Keating, R., Nubian Twilight Harcourt, Brace & World 1963

Kidd, B., Documents Illustrative of the History of the Church Vol. II Soc. for Promoting Christian Knowledge 1922

King, A., Quotations in Black Greenwood Press 1981

Kristeller, P., Renaissance Thought and Its Sources Columbia 1979

Livingstone, E., The Oxford Dictionary of the Christian Church Oxford Univ. 1997

MacMullen, R., Christianizing the Roman Empire Yale Univ. 1984

Malcioln, J., The African Origins of Modern Judaism Africa World Press 1996

Africa's Indispensable Role

Marcus, H., A History of Ethiopia Univ. of Calif. 1994

Marshall, T., The Glorious Martyrdom of St. Cyprian Canterbury Tales (net)

Mayor, J., & Souter, A., O Septimi Florentis Tertvlliani Apologeticvs: Tertullian's Apology Cambridge Univ. 1917

Metzger, B., The Early Version of the New Testament Clarendon Press 1977 & Oxford Press 1987

Millar, F., The Emperor in the Roman World Cornell Univ. Press 1977

Misri, I., The Story of the Copts Middle East Council of Churches 1978

Munro-Hay, S., Aksum: An African Civilization of Late Antiquity Munro-Hay 1991

Oates, W., Basic Writings of Saint Augustine Random House 1948

O'leary, D., The Saints of Egypt The Macmillan Co. 1937

Parrinder, G., Religion in Africa Penguin 1955

Bibliography

Perowne, S., Roman Mythology Bedrick Books 1983

Pfeffer, L., Church, State, and Freedom Beacon Press 1953

Radice, B., Letters, and Penegyricus Vol. I - II Cambridge - Harvard Univ. 1969

Richardson, D., & O'Brien, K., Egypt: A Rough Guide Rough Guides 1993

Robinson, C., Conversion of Europe Longman, Green & Co. 1917

Rogers, J.A., Sex and Race Rogers Publ. 1967

Schwartz, W., Principles and Problems of Biblical Translation Cambridge Univ. 1955

Seldes, G., The Great Quotations Pocket Books 1960, 1967

Shinnie, P., Meroe Praeger 1967

Simons, G., Barbarian Europe Timelife 1968

Smith, W., Dictionary of Greek and Roman Biography and Mythology Murray 1902

Africa's Indispensable Role

Sykes, E., Everyman's Dictionary of Non-classical Mythology Dutton & Sons 1952

Tacitus, P., & Church, A. Tr. & Brodribb, W. Tr., Histories ebooks@Adelaide 2009

Taylor, J., Egypt and Nubia British Museum 1991

Thompson, C., Septuagint Bible Falcon Wing Press 1954

Tompkins, P., The Magic of Obelisks Harper & Row 1981

Trigg, J., Origen Knox Press 1983

Von Balthasar, H., Origen: Spirit and Fire Catholic Univ. Press 1984

Von Ranke, L., A History of England Vol. I A.M.S. Press 1980

Walker, B., The Woman's Encyclopedia of Myths and Secrets Rodeo Press 1981

Ward, P., A Dictionary of Common Fallacies Prometheus Books 1989

Weiss, J., Earliest Christianity: A History of the Period A.D. 30 - 150 Vol. II Harper Bros. 1937

Bibliography

Wellard, J., Lost Worlds of Africa Dutton 1967

Windsor, R., From Babylon to Timbuktu Exposition Press 1969

Worthy, R.L., YHSVH KornerStone Books 2008

_____., Behind the Veil: Nuns Nat. Film Board of Canada 1984

_____., Collier's Encyclopedia Macmillan 1986

_____., Dictionary of African Biography Reference Publ. 1977

_____., Dictionary of the Middle Ages Vol. X Scribner & Sons 1988

_____., Encyclopedia of Philosophy Macmillan Freepress 1973

_____., Encyclopedia of Religion Macmillan 1987

_____., Grolier Multimedia Encyclopedia Grolier 1997

_____., Historical Dictionary of Ethiopia and Eritrea Scarecrow Press 1994

Africa's Indispensable Role

_____., Illustrated Dictionary & Concordance of the Bible Jerusalem Publ. House 1986

_____., Marcus Aurelius and His Times Black Inc. 1945

_____., The American Peoples Encyclopedia Spencer Press 1955

_____., The Gnostic Scriptures Doubleday & Co. 1987

_____., The Lost Books of the Bible and the Forgotten Books of Eden Bell 1979

_____., The New Catholic Encyclopedia Heraty 1967, 1981

_____., The New Columbia Encyclopedia Columbia Press 1975

_____., The World Book Encyclopedia World Book Inc. 1970 - 2003

_____., Universal Standard Encyclopedia W. Funk 1955

John the Baptist

Africa's Indispensable Role

A

Abun	47, 48, 113	Aristeas	26
Adam	80, 111	Arius	67, 75, 95
Afonso Mendez	114	Ark of the Covenant	28, 104
Afse	109	Athanasius	44, 45, 47, 67, 72, 77, 78
Ahura Mazda	85	Athengoras	12
Akhenaten	2	Athens	85
Alemanni	89	Augustine	xiv, 3, 79, 80, 81, 82, 83, 120, 121
Alexander the Great	26	Augustus	39
Alexandros	77	Axum	46, 49, 106, 112
Alwa	106, 107		
Ammun	69, 70		

B

Anatolia	xi, 2	Babylon	91
Anianus	8	Balkans	40
Anra Mainyut	85	Belgica	40
Antoniyos (*Monastery*)	68	Benedict	72
Antony	66, 67, 68	Blemmye	105
Aramaic	89	Britons	111
		Bucalis	10, 21
		Bulan (King)	89

Index

C

Caecilian 77
78
Caesar 35
36, 37, 38, 39, 60
Canaanite 15
32, 45, 72
Carthage xi
19, 22, 39, 53, 54, 57, 58,
77, 78, 79, 81, 82, 83, 120
Carthaginian
Gods 54
Catacombs 18
19, 21
Catechetical
Institute 12
13, 15, 16, 62, 63, 89
Cato 35
Caucasian ix
xi
Chaldeans 56
Charlemagne 86
87
Chester Beatty
Papyrus 29
30

Christ vii
xiv, 2, 3, 7, 10, 16, 21, 27,
28, 44, 52, 53, 55, 64, 66,
75, 76, 80, 96, 112, 118,
122, 126
Churches
(*Ancient*) xiv
10, 21, 22, 49, 50, 107, 108,
109, 117
Cicero 35
Clement 12
13, 14, 15, 62, 89, 90
Clovis 89
Constantine I 7
74, 77, 88, 90, 91, 92, 93,
94, 95, 96, 97, 98, 99, 100
Constantius 94
Copts 5
9, 13, 14, 16, 20, 21, 29, 30,
33, 39, 48, 72, 113, 117
Cosmas
Indicopleustes 109
Council
of Arles 95
Council
of Carthage 82
Council
of Nicea 75
95
Crispus 94
Crusades 116

Africa's Indispensable Role

Cyprian	22	Donatist Controversy	77
58, 59, 60, 61		78, 95	
Cyrenaica	9	Dorians	83
10, 32, 83		Dragon	152
		Druids	86

D

Dacia	94
Darada, D.	9
44, 47	
David	20
21	
Debra Damo	49
109	
Decius	37
38	
Demetrius	15
18, 21, 63	
Devil	57
67, 152	
Dhu Nuwas	107
Didymus	15
Dies Solis	97
Diocletian	xiii
33, 37, 38, 69, 77, 105	

E

Edict of Milan	90
Ela Abreha II	48
49	
Ela Asbeha	108
Ela Asfeha	48
49	
Ela Shahel II	48
49	
Elamites	85
86	
Elephant In the Room	vii
118	
Endelechius	74
England	13
111, 116	
Epictetus	85

141

Index

Epiphanius	65
Essenes	4
Etruria	35
Eumanius	12
Eurysthenes	83
Eusebius	40
44, 47	
Ezana (*Aezanes*)	46
47, 48	
Ezekiel	45

F

Fausta	95
Felicitas	53
Felix of Apthungi	77
Flamen	34
Forum	102
Franks	89
French	117
Frumentius	44
45, 46, 47, 48, 113	

G

Galerius Maximus	59
60	
Garsemot IV (Queen)	9
44, 47	
Gathas	85
Gaul	40
Ge'ez	48
Gelasius	73
George	50
152	
Germany	40
87, 110, 111, 116	
Gnostics	55
Goths	77
Greece	2
15, 88	
Gregory of Tours	89
Gregory Thaumaturus	xi
66	

142

Africa's Indispensable Role

H

Ham	x
Hebrews	viii
ix, xi, 2, 4, 9, 21, 26, 27, 28, 35, 36, 56, 60, 63, 89, 91, 97, 104	
Helena	94
95	
Herodotus	2
Hexapla	65
Hippo	3
79, 80, 83	
Horus	105

I

Illyria (*Albania*)	75
Inquisition	116
Isis	105
Islam	113
Israel	3
4, 5, 9	
Italy	40

J

Jacobite	113
Jerome	65
109	
Jerusalem	4
35, 45, 104, 116	
John	3
150	
John the Baptist	21
138	
Joseph	x
Jupiter	73
Justinian	107
Justus	12

K

Kaleb (King)	107
108	
Kebra Negast	104
Khazars	89
Kizhi Monastery	41

Index

L

Lalibela 50
109, 111
Language Chart 122
Leonidas 62
Leontius 77
Licinius 91
Logos 62
Lost Books
of the Bible 27
28, 60
Luke 38
Lycopolis
(*Assuit*) 71

M

Madonna 64
112
Makuria 106
107
Mani 79
80
Marcus
Aurelius 85
91
Marianus 12

Mark 7
8, 9, 10, 12, 15, 21, 41, 148, 149
Marriage 111
Martyrologium
Romanum 119
Mary 64
76, 112
Matthew 30
Maxentius 88
Maximian 94
Medhave
Alem 109
111
Melchiades 73
Menologion
of Basil II xi
Milan 79
Mithra 85
86
Monotheism 2
3
Moses viii
ix, x, 97, 111

N

Namphamo 32

Africa's Indispensable Role

Nero	36, 38, 60	Pantaneus	12, 13, 14, 15
Nestor	100, 101	Paul	x, 30, 82, 125, 151
Nicene Creed	76, 77	Pelagian Doctrine	82
Nitria	70	Pentateuch	24, 25, 26
Nobatae	105, 106, 107	Perpetua	52, 53, 54
Nubia	43	Persia	101
Numidia	32, 79, 83, 113	Peter	58
		Petros	38
		Philip	9, 44

O

		Phoenicia	xi, 45, 56
Origen	15, 55, 62, 63, 64, 65, 66	Phrygia	72
Osiris	105	Pilate	28, 76
Oxyrhynchus	71	Pinikir	85
		Pispir	67
		Pomerania	116
		Pontifex Maximus	35, 73, 91, 98

P

Pacome	69, 70, 71	Pope	73, 74, 113, 114
Palamon	70	Portugal	113, 114
Palestine	2		
Pantalewon	109		

Index

Ptolemies 26
32

Q

Qulzum 67
68

R

Ra 85
Rhaetia 40
Roha 111
Roman Deities 34
Russia 40
41
Rylands Papyrus 25

S

Sabbath 96
97, 114
Sawya (Queen) 47
Saxons 86
87

Sayzana (*Shaiazana*) 47
48
Scandinavia 111
116
Seneca 85
Septimius Severus 36
73, 102
Septuagint 24
25, 26, 27
Sheba (Queen) 104
Simeon (Monastery) xiv
Simon 55
Sol Invictus 92
Solomon 104
111
Stoicism 85
Synesius 83

T

Tabennisi 70
Tacitus 3
Tagaste 79
Tertullian 37
39, 54, 55, 56, 57, 63, 96

Africa's Indispensable Role

Teutonic	111
Thecla	72
Theodora	94
Theodosius	100, 101
Thomas	93
Titus	39
Torah	24, 25
Trajan	36, 38, 39
Trinity	56

U

V

Valerian	37, 38, 60
Vandals	83
Victor I	73
Victoria	69

W

X

Y

Yared	109
Yeshaq	109
YHSVH (see Christ)	
YHVH	76, 93, 97, 122
Yohannes	72

Z

Zamik-el	109
Zarathushtra (Zoroaster)	85
Zeno	85
Zervan Akarana	85
Zoroastrianism	85

Tribute

This wonderful painting is of Africa's Saint Mark the Evangelist! It was painted by the Greek artist Emmanuel Tzanes in 1657 CE. Today it is kept in the Benaki Museum. That all notwithstanding, had it not been for the Apostle Mark's first century determination, and the devotion of his loyal African followers, the Christian Religion might well have failed to survive on the earth, because of the vehement persecution of the world's first Christians, by the emperors of the Roman Empire.

Africa's Indispensable Role

A. I. R. - Notes

Love not the World, or the things of the World—for any man who loves the World, the love of the Father is not in him . . .

Saint John

So, what have we learned? It is a mistake to trust the untrustable . . .

A. I. R. - Notes

Do not be conformed to this world, but be transformed by the renewing of your mind . . .

Saint Paul

Oh' and finally – Africa's Role is Indispensable!

Africa's Indispensable Role

It is manifest: There is truth, and then there's all the rest . . .

www.ingramcontent.com/pod-product-compliance
Lightning Source LLC
Chambersburg PA
CBHW051935160426
43198CB00013B/2160